Praise for
Embodied Activism

"As a result of silencing the voice of our bodies, we as activists unknowingly per-petuate the oppressive systems we seek to transform. In a mind-centric, product-driven society that socializes us to not only ignore but deny that our bodies are a vital source of information about the impact of the world through which we move, Johnson invites us to slow down and . . . feel the issues of social injustice in our bodies rather than just talking about them, to listen deeply to what's going on inside us so that we can learn to be fully present with ourselves and others."

—LISA JO EPSTEIN, PhD, executive and artistic director at Just Act

"A soulful yet practical guide to personal and political change. Johnson deftly avoids the trap of reducing embodiment to a 'tool' or set of mechanical systems for producing 'emotion regulation,' instead gently insisting on a view of the body as a living organism of deep beauty and complexity. Organizers, change-makers, counselors, and coaches will find Johnson's frameworks and exercises immedi-ately applicable to their practice while scholars and theory lovers will thrill at the rich depth and texture presented here. This book is a treasure."

—KAI CHENG THOM, MSW, MSc, author of *I Hope We Choose Love*

"This wonderful, profoundly empowering, and highly accessible book is a must-read for anyone engaged in the work of liberation and social change, or anyone who has a body."

—NICK WALKER, PhD, author of *Neuroqueer Heresies*

"Deeply situated within larger systemic justice work, this book offers accessible practices to reclaim, heal, and catalyze our particular body stories to more fully embody the work of social transformation. A 'must-read' that will quickly become an important companion in our embodied work for liberation."

—BETH BERILA, PhD, author of *Integrating Mindful-ness into Anti-Oppression Pedagogy*

embodied activism

engaging the body to cultivate liberation, justice, and authentic connection

A PRACTICAL GUIDE FOR TRANSFORMATIVE SOCIAL CHANGE

rae johnson, phd

FOREWORD BY BAYO AKOMOLAFE, PHD

North Atlantic Books
Huichin, unceded Ohlone land
aka Berkeley, California

"Small Kindness" by Danusha Laméris reprinted with permission of University of Pittsburgh Press.

Published by
North Atlantic Books
Huichin, unceded Ohlone land
aka Berkeley, California

Cover art © Talashow via Getty Images
Cover design by Amanda Weiss
Book design by Happenstance Type-O-Rama

Printed in Canada

Embodied Activism: Engaging the Body to Cultivate Liberation, Justice, and Authentic Connection—A Practical Guide for Transformative Social Change is sponsored and published by North Atlantic Books, an educational nonprofit based in the unceded Ohlone land Huichin (*aka* Berkeley, CA) that collaborates with partners to develop cross-cultural perspectives; nurture holistic views of art, science, the humanities, and healing; and seed personal and global transformation by publishing work on the relationship of body, spirit, and nature.

CONTENT DISCLAIMER: The following information is intended for general information purposes only. Individuals should always see their health care provider before administering any suggestions made in this book. Any application of the material set forth in the following pages is at the reader's discretion and is their sole responsibility.

North Atlantic Books' publications are distributed to the US trade and internationally by Penguin Random House Publisher Services. For further information, visit our website at www.northatlanticbooks.com.

Library of Congress Cataloging-in-Publication Data

Names: Johnson, Rae, author.
Title: Embodied activism: Engaging the Body to Cultivate Liberation, Justice, and Authentic Connection—A Practical Guide for Social change / Rae Johnson; foreword by Bayo Akomolafe, Ph.D.
Description: Berkeley, California: North Atlantic Books, [2023] | Includes bibliographical references and index.
Identifiers: LCCN 2022036283 (print) | LCCN 2022036284 (ebook) | ISBN 9781623176990 (trade paperback) | ISBN 9781623177003 (ebook)
Subjects: LCSH: Body language—Social aspects. | Human body—Social aspects. | Body image—Social aspects. | Social justice.
Classification: LCC BF637.N66 J649 2023 (print) | LCC BF637.N66 (ebook) | DDC 153.6/9—dc23/eng/20230110
LC record available at https://lccn.loc.gov/2022036283
LC ebook record available at https://lccn.loc.gov/2022036284

1 2 3 4 5 6 7 8 9 MARQUIS 28 27 26 25 24 23

Contents

Foreword

Forgive me.

I have a confession: I have little use for the term *social justice,* or its theoretical corollary, *activism.*

Let me explain . . . since it might already start to feel a bit awkward to express reservations about these closely related concepts in the foreword of a book that focuses on their relationship.

It's simple, really: I don't trust "social justice." Not yet. Perhaps not ever. There's too much it hides away, circumvents, and leaves out in its palpable desire to speak straightforwardly, to speak truth to power. *To win.*

Instead of being something that could be known in advance, something already predetermined and given, social justice appears to be an effect of a public order that is largely calibrated to a politics of recognition and representation; to the centrality of voice; to the hope that human agency might challenge and ultimately alter oppressive structures that constrain its freedoms; to the flat instrumentality of the nonhuman world around us; to the phallic spectacularity of victory; and to the properness of the citizen-subject. It seems less a way of bringing to light the painful exclusions of an uneven society than a mechanism for the coproduction of subjects and certain kinds of subjectivities, heavily indebted to the paradigms it performs resistance to. More of an instrument of subjugation and subjectivization than a road to new worlds.

I write this as a West African son, brother, father, writer, teacher, and recipient of a brand of social justice that at one time required my people to turn away from their own bodies, from their own histories, and from the local imperatives around them. I grew up in schizophrenic lands, torn between the stickiness of a past that lingered and the futures our colonial masters (and their guns) enforced. I grew up in the sweltering heat of many power outages, stinging hisses followed by that sinking feeling of abandonment and collective moans about how our country had failed us, how the gods no longer heard our prayers. Outside our windows, a derelict cemetery fanned out into the horizons—the same cemetery where we had buried justice and its cousins.

At one time, we, too, marched under the banner of justice. Some still do. We protested the injustices of our colonial masters. We hated how they treated us. A woman named Madame Nwanyeruwa spat in the face of one Mark Emeruwa, a census officer of the British colonial government in eastern Nigeria, who had come to count her and her chickens for tax purposes. "Was your own mother counted?" she asked, fire spilling from her eyes. Her question ignited the Aba Women's War of 1929, short decades after a British punitive expedition had invaded the ancient city of Benin, ransacked the palace, incarcerated the king, and stolen spiritual artifacts that now sit in Western museums today under the collective appellation of the "Benin Bronzes." In the years that followed Madame Nwanyeruwa's defiance, we would chase away the British, completing our claims to national independence as the lowered Union Jack sailed our winds for the last time in 1960.

But by winning the game, we became part of the game: we raised our own flags and relegated our languages to second-tier status in a bid to keep up with new international benchmarks for *development*. We adopted the powdered wigs of eighteenth-century European nobility as emblems of justice in our newly furnished courts of law and imported "universal" psychologies and Western therapies that proved ineffective within our cultural domains. Justice meant adopting the inclusive paradigms of our former lords—whether it was the World Bank's structural adjustment program or the normative assumptions of the American Left—even if that also meant accepting the violence tucked into the new quotidian. Even if this left a sore aftertaste on our tongues. If it was American, it was good, we assured ourselves.

Not much has changed.

We haven't gotten very far at mimicking colonial worlds, despite our many attempts. We can neither return to an original Indigeneity nor march headfirst into some just future awaiting us. The past has changed, and the future is not for us. There's not much to the notion of justice when you are stuck in a temporality where you are always late.

Somewhere in the tensile stretch of collective imagination, we still recognize the irony of our postcolonial victories. We are tired of rumors about tomorrow's revolution, exhausted with balancing on vanishing threads of hope—our labors for something better, something else, eaten up by the scorching sun. If one answer to the riddle of Theseus's ship is a persuasive invitation to see the world processually, to notice that everything that claims identity and presence is but a trace of its reiterative ongoingness and flow, then might it not be said that the unforgiving sociality that lends its name to "social justice" and extracts from us a cruel optimism is a performative rehearsal of the slave plantation? Constantly navigating the thick and intensely Black geographies that subsidize the Euro-American-global public order (the hidden, dissonant underground of the public), we whisper to ourselves that even justice doesn't love us. Even justice gets in the way of the transformations we seek.

What do you do when your attempts to flee your prison are a feature of your imprisonment? Where do you turn when your blood-purchased victories do things you don't expect them to do? How does one speak truth to power when one's lips are misshapen? How does one speak straightforwardly when the very act of speaking fortifies the foundations of power upon which the Man might plant his claims to our bodies? Can I trust a sociality that leaves out the generous sweep of my *long body,* the ghostly entrails of my manifold tentacularities that stretch deep into deep time, and seditiously into the more-than-human? Can I trust a justice that gives me a seat at the table but forbids me access to the wilds outside the building? Can I trust a justice that urges me to raise my head in the morning, and kneels on my neck in the evening?

You see, *social justice*—at least the iteration of it that has fallen prey to my people's scrutiny—doesn't quite do the work it could be doing.

Something about the epistemology of contemporary activism seems to coincide with the recognizably modern assumptions of totalizing arrival, full capture, and complete articulation. As if it were possible to contain emergence, to satisfy a full archive of longings. It is almost as if activism resonates with the urban conditions that secrete it, desiring the spectacular, wanting to square both sides of the equation. But the logic of its exertions subtly reinscribes and fortifies the walls it wants to pull down. Sometimes the antagonism of resistance is already anticipated in the departmental policies of the resisted.

If nothing else sinks in here, in the shock of an admission is why I am suspicious of the practices hidden behind the Euro-American label of social justice: I desire a way out. I am tired. *We* are tired. We are fed up. We want to fly—not to utopian arrangements but to new possibilities for becoming response-able. We want to inhabit new sites of power with the world, with the corporeal vocations of our bodies often invisibilized by the overwhelming language of the pixelated social.

With this book, Rae Johnson tends to my restless spirits. Or rather, Rae invites them into the textual-spiritual-pragmatic touch of a gentle massage. Accompanied by tea. Spirits love a good massage. And tea.

This book moves with the immediacy of touch. Coming *to* touch and coming *in* touch are its beating veins, pulsating with sensuous rhythms. Addressing the social reductionisms that treat activism as a hyperprofessionalized sphere of acting that opens its gates to a few while excluding the many, and which requires a surgical excision of the material body, of the everyday, Rae takes a deep dive into the intelligence of our own bodies—no longer relegated to the backdrop of politics but the very heart of it. Sinews. Sighs. Tendons. And thighs. Yes, *that body*. Not a lyrical Vitruvian imagination of it.

The case made on these pages is that we may have mistaken activism for an increasingly stereotypic and limited set of disembodied outcomes and ideals. Could it be that the work to address the pernicious effects of, say, racism invites not just protests and legislation, not just senators and their proposals, but grandmothers and hot soup? Breathing exercises and dance? Are there ways of mapping resilience that bring us home to our bodies? Could becoming accountable and becoming response-able refer to a spectrum of practices that brings in more actors and agencies than we've ever dreamed admissible?

When Rae Johnson writes that "it is not difficult to understand how activist spaces may come to embody the very qualities of society they consciously disavow," they position themselves at the great chiasmus of a material turn in things that now infects our transdisciplinary conversations. If, in the words of Karen Barad, we have given language and the social too much power, this is a time for a somatic descent into embodiment—one that does not abandon the social but queers it by fastening its spirited Icarusian wings to the Daedalusian discipline of the body, long denied its say in what matters and what comes to matter. This is what this book does: it brings the moral arc of the universe that presumably bends toward justice down to earth and locates it within our bodies in their somatic-semiotic richness.

Look through these pages if you are as tired as I am, as my people are. Look through it if you sense that what's on the menu of things to do is a lot more than has been popularly published. Indeed, this book is part of that expanded menu.

When Greek mathematician Archimedes of Syracuse, entranced by the beauty of his own calculations, said, "Give me a lever long enough and a fulcrum on which to place it, and I shall move the world," he spoke with the cadence of one floating above the elements—which is why eons later, Africa's foremost and most celebrated novelist, Chinua Achebe, formulated (in his book *No Longer at Ease*) a gracious response to Archimedes' request: "Such a place does not exist. We all have to stand on the earth itself and go with her at her pace."

Go with her at her pace. I cannot think of a more fitting invitation to embodiment, to an embodied activism, to the intelligence of the corporeal, than those words—as I cannot think of a more gracious host of these convenings than Rae Johnson.

I trust I am now forgiven.

BAYO AKOMOLAFE, PhD
Chennai, India
Author, These Wilds beyond our Fences:
Letters to My Daughter on Humanity's Search for Home

Preface

When I wrote *Embodied Social Justice* several years ago, I knew that my next book needed to take the ideas and insights from that book and make them accessible to a broader audience. Where *Embodied Social Justice* was aimed at a professional audience—therapists, teachers, community leaders, and frontline workers in the human services—*Embodied Activism* is written for everyone and anyone who has ever wanted to make a change in the world. Whether you're a seasoned activist or brand new to social change work, I hope the ideas, stories, and exercises in this book help you find your feet and your voice in a new way.

Writing this book not only provided an opportunity to highlight the practical and experiential aspects of my work; it also allowed me to weave together the emerging ideas of a growing community of social change agents who understand embodiment and social justice as inextricably connected. Where there once were a few bright, clear voices insisting that there could be no justice without the body, there is now a resounding chorus. The need for this perspective is perhaps greater and more urgent than ever, and I'm delighted to include many of these new voices in the pages of this book.

A fundamental premise of *Embodied Activism* is that injustice is about the misuse of power, wherever and however it shows up. As I navigate my own shifting social locations and intersecting social identifications, it has been essential to write from a place that acknowledges my cultures, privileges, and hardships while also recognizing that power infuses everything. It seeps into my body, infiltrates my thinking, and complexifies my interactions in ways that are impossible to sort into neat categories of social difference. Writing this book has helped me to focus more on my embodied use of power than on my membership in particular social groups. My hope for *Embodied Activism* is that it offers readers an opportunity to interrogate and shape how power shows up for them—in their bodies and in their lives.

Acknowledgments

The first inklings of this book appeared during an informal talk that Christine Caldwell and I offered to somatic psychology students in the fall of 2017. Perched on a meditation cushion in a classroom at Naropa University, I wondered aloud about microactivism and what it might look like if we brought an embodied perspective to it. Following our talk, copies of my handwritten speaking notes made their way into the student grapevine and became the seed for many fruitful conversations. I am indebted to Christine for always being such a wonderful coconspirator, and to Diane Israel for asking if she could share my speaking notes with others. Diane's enthusiasm for the work was infectious, and her bright spark at Naropa and in my life is dearly missed.

My deep appreciation goes out to Nkem Ndefo, codeveloper of an online course on embodied activism that helped me crystallize my thinking on the topic. Having a thought partner of Nkem's caliber is a rare pleasure, and the enthusiastic student response to our course affirmed there was an audience for a book. More recently, working with the training team of the Relational Somatic Healing program allowed me to share some of the ideas and practices from the book while it was still being written. My thanks to Shirley Dvir, developer of the Relational Somatic Healing model, for immediately grasping what an embodied activism was all about and how it could shape the way we work with groups and teams.

To Niki Koumoutsos, Kaleb Sinclair, Sean Ambrose, Christine Caldwell, and Sam Grant, thank you so much for being willing to be interviewed for this book, and for your insight, transparency, and generosity of spirit. The wisdom gleaned from your explorations into embodied activism has enriched the book and continues to inspire me. My gratitude also to Maya, Alex, Ayesha, and the many others who shared their body stories with me.

Lastly, sincere thanks to Keith Donnell, my editor at North Atlantic Books, who approached me about writing a book just when my ideas about embodied activism were ready for harvesting. Your timing was perfect.

1

Reconsidering, Reframing, and Retooling

patterns in the flesh

many of us are in the kind of existential pain
that Douglas Adams once described
as the *long dark tea-time of the soul.*
icebergs melt and wildfires blaze
violence escalates, viruses replicate
lifelong activists for social and environmental justice
speak in terms of "hospice care"
for the species and the planet.
with the world simultaneously
burning and drowning
it might seem like nothing we do
will matter very much in the end.
but what if nothing
could be further from the truth?
what if it's not only what matters in the end
but what matters in the spacious now

—here, in the short arc of history.
not just the what
but the how.
not just the big picture
but noticing that the big picture
is created by patterns on the small scale
in the warmth of our flesh.

As global conditions galvanize us to transform increasingly untenable social systems, it can be difficult to know how to engage effectively in support of liberation, justice, and authentic connection. The amount of sustained effort required for real change may feel unsupportable, and the benefits intangible or easily eroded. How do ordinary people with demanding lives find the bandwidth and the footholds to leverage our actions so that we make a meaningful difference in the world? Where are the handholds to engage with others in ways that don't inadvertently perpetuate disconnection, misunderstanding, or harm? Is there a way to stay centered and grounded as we take on overwhelmingly complex issues and navigate charged relational territories? What does it take to live our values within social systems that lack a moral center?

Part of the challenge we face stems from how many of us have been taught to understand social change—for example, that it mostly occurs at the level of laws and institutions and is largely undertaken by politicians, lobbyists, and expert activists. We may also be directing our efforts mainly at changing the opinions, beliefs, and attitudes of others. This book introduces a very different approach to social change: one that focuses on how politics are embedded in our everyday experiences and enacted through our relationships with others. And instead of thinking about justice as a process that starts with changing people's minds or superficial behaviors, this approach understands our bodies—how we feel in them, and how we relate to others through them—as a crucial site of transformative intervention. *Embodied Activism* proposes a radical revisioning of activism that places our everyday embodied experience of power relations at the center of our change efforts. Drawing on the creativity of innovative thought leaders and the wisdom of ancient traditions around the world, it describes a process of reclaiming our sensual engagement with the world around us and articulates how we might harness that engagement for social repair and transformation.

Reconsidering Social Change

Poet and activist Audre Lorde once asserted that "the master's tools will never dismantle the master's house," observing how entrenched systems of power consistently resist real change unless and until radically different interventions are deployed. Other activists maintain that many kinds of protest don't work over the long term because they are founded on assumptions about democracy that no longer apply—for example, the assumption that if enough people communicate a clear and consistent message, it will be taken up by those in power. Still others claim that some forms of collective action aren't sufficiently inclusive. Antipoverty activists point out that boycotts fail to include the economically disenfranchised, and disability justice activists argue that many rallies and protest marches are inaccessible to members of their community.

Even when activism results in noticeable success—in the case of marriage for same-sex couples, for instance—the insidiousness of the repercussions can be disheartening. Now that being gay is more publicly acceptable in many countries, queer liberation community organizers struggle against a tide of corporate "pinkwashing"[1] intended to capture a growing LGBTQIA+ market and obscure the harm still being done by implicitly cisheterosexist organizations, institutions, and governments. After all the hard-won progress on civil and human rights, the resurgence of anti-Black racism and increasingly authoritarian forms of government can feel like a disheartening "one step forward, two steps back" dance with intractable forces of domination and violence.

Beyond the sometimes-glacial pace of social change in an era when actual glaciers are melting faster than ever, there are deeper issues with current forms of activism besides their long-term effectiveness. One of the most concerning is the high levels of burnout experienced among those who dedicate their lives to making a better world for everyone. Social movement scholars argue that burnout— the almost unavoidable deterioration of physical and emotional well-being due to participating in activism—is a persistent impediment to sustaining social movements.[2] Whether this burnout is understood as a consequence of caring too much or being targeted too often, when it reaches a critical tipping point, many activists have little choice but to abandon their involvement in the very causes they once devoted their lives to. The resulting lack of sustained leadership within a movement can create fragmentation, loss of momentum, and an overall erosion of hope and goodwill.

The harsh toll that activism takes on the bodies and spirits of activists may also reflect an underlying misalignment between the tactics activists employ and their desired outcome of a more just and compassionate world. In their book *Joyful Militancy,* longtime activists Nick Montgomery and carla bergman articulate some of the within-movement causes of burnout related to how activists treat one another. Referred to as *rigid radicalism,* the scapegoating, competitiveness, intolerance, mistrust, and adherence to dogma that are hallmarks of oppressive social systems also show up in many activist communities.[3] Unfortunately, these characteristics of rigid radicalism help to shape public perception of activists and activism as well.

At the same time, it is not difficult to understand how activist spaces may come to embody the very qualities of society they consciously disavow. When so much collective action is fueled by justified outrage, how do activists make space for joy and care? When the world is on fire, how do activists take time to breathe? When so much effort is mobilized toward achieving a particular goal, what happens to process and relationship? When survival depends upon a critical analysis of overwhelmingly oppressive conditions, how do we keep our politics from focusing more on destruction than creation?

These questions are not intended to suggest that current ways of engaging in activism aren't effective at all or that the project of social change should be abandoned as futile or irreparably flawed. It's essential to recognize the dedication, sacrifice, and ingenuity that have helped to secure the rights and freedoms so many of us currently enjoy. And in considering the possibilities offered by a shift toward process, relationship, and pleasure, it's important not to cast fierceness, perseverance, and being goal-oriented as oppositional rather than complementary qualities. Rather, pointing out the challenges and limitations of the existing paradigm of social change is intended to help illuminate how activism might be refined, expanded, and reconsidered.

What Does an Activist Look Like?

One of the first tasks in this revisioning is to unpack and open up prevailing notions of what constitutes activism and what an activist looks like. When you imagine an activist, perhaps you visualize someone on the street carrying a sign and shouting into a bullhorn or holding a candle at a vigil. Or perhaps you think of people working together to organize boycotts, circulate petitions, or engage in legislative lobbying. These examples illustrate a form of activism that works to put pressure on social systems by identifying an injustice and demanding change. In this scenario, the primary actors are often people on the front lines, and the primary target is typically an organization or government. But if we broaden the definition of activism by boiling it down to its most basic core— any intentional action taken with the goal of positive social change—then other forms of activism become available for our consideration.

Deepa Iyer's mapping of roles in a social change ecosystem highlights some additional ways of being an activist.[4] While those who serve as community organizers and frontline responders may be the most visible players, there are other equally crucial roles: the caregivers who nourish and sustain community members, the storytellers who craft and preserve the legacy of struggle, and the healers who tend to the collective intergenerational trauma caused by oppressive social conditions. According to Iyer, one of the keys to effective and sustainable activism is to engage in a process of ongoing self-reflection that helps to identify the roles that best suit one's temperament and leverage one's strengths.

Another feature of the activist stereotype is someone who works extensively with others and is enlivened by being part of a group or community—in other words, an extrovert. This focus on group interaction can be challenging for introverts, who may prefer working alone or with just a few others. Sara Corbett, a self-described introvert activist, notes that quiet activities like writing letters or making crafts can provide an opportunity for deep-thinking introverts to have their voices heard.[5]

Corbett challenges another stereotype about activism as well: that to be effective, one must direct outrage at those perpetrating the injustice. Instead of adopting a "shaming and shouting" approach, she advocates for quiet actions that appeal to the better natures of those in power. For example, a group that Corbett was working with launched a campaign that involved sending handmade handkerchiefs to the board members of Marks & Spencer, a large UK-based retail chain, to persuade them to pay employees a living wage. These gifts were followed by hand-delivered cards celebrating Valentine's Day and Christmas. Within ten months, the organization announced the implementation of a living wage policy. For Corbett, the quiet intimacy of a one-to-one personal touch made the difference in this campaign and demonstrated the effectiveness of "introvert activism."

Some social change agents might not necessarily even identify as activists or understand their work to be activism. But this doesn't mean their efforts don't make a big (and sometimes crucial) impact on social movements or political issues. For example, the role of art in activism has a long and impressive history. The antiwar experimental art of the 1920s Dadaist movement in Berlin, Mexican muralists protesting for worker protection, African American civil rights documentary photography, Vietnam war protest anthems of the 1960s, and the feminist performance art of the anonymous gorilla-masked Guerilla Girls are just a few examples. Augusto Boal's Theater of the Oppressed harnesses dramatic techniques to examine everyday issues of injustice, and dance as activism has a long and vibrant history that continues to this day.[6]

Stephen Duncombe and Steve Lambert with the Center for Artistic Activism say art can play a crucial role in social change efforts.[7] Duncombe and Lambert note that most activism is focused on creating an *effect*—for example, the effect of changing an unjust social norm, policy, or law. On the other hand, they say, art occupies itself primarily with generating *affect*—eliciting a particular emotion, such as compassion, outrage, or pride. Artistic activism harnesses the power of creative feeling and brings it together with the directed intention of social action. Recognizing artists as activists opens up another facet of an unnecessarily limiting stereotype of what an activist looks like.

Activism also occurs in another (perhaps surprising) corner of the social world—among academic researchers.[8] Although the term *researcher* might conjure images of someone in a white lab coat conducting experiments in a university laboratory, many researchers do important work that looks nothing like our preconceived notions. Across a wide range of academic disciplines—including anthropology, education, gender studies, psychology, and critical race studies—activist researchers work to help the world better understand the root causes of inequality, suffering, and systemic violence by illuminating the lived experiences of those who experience these injustices. Working alongside these communities, activist researchers develop strategies for transforming oppressive conditions by using their investigative and analytic skills in the service of social change.

As the preceding examples suggest, activism is as varied and creative as the humans who engage in it. Although organized community action in the form of boycotts, information campaigns, strikes, vigils, and public protests will always be an important tool in stirring up what renowned civil rights activist John Lewis called "good trouble," expanding our vision of what an activist looks like can encourage deeper, broader, and more diverse participation in the collective work of changing the world.

Where Does Activism Occur?

Although systems of oppression are never about individuals per se, individual effort can and does make a difference in changing those systems. And while we may not have created the conditions of oppression that currently exist, our failure to resist these systems of oppression effectively maintains the status quo. Once an oppressive system is established, all it needs to thrive is our passive willingness to go along. So the second task in reframing activism is to diversify its locations. Even in the examples above, the actions described focus mostly on change at the level of communities, organizations, legislation, or policy. While these large-scale efforts target important arenas of public life, those aren't the only places where meaningful change occurs. In other words, revisioning activism requires unpacking how social systems work by analyzing their related and interconnected dimensions.

Social systems can be understood as functioning simultaneously on three interrelated levels: the *macro* level of government and social institutions, the *meso* level of organizations and communities, and the *micro* level of individuals and small groups. As members of a society, we are socialized through interactions at all three levels and across multiple social roles and identities. These interactions teach us, explicitly and implicitly, the "rules" governing allowable behavior and acceptable characteristics. In our families, classrooms, jobs, and communities, we learn what is considered okay (and *who* is considered okay) by those who hold power, such as our parents, teachers, bosses, clergy, police, and politicians. These social norms are articulated and maintained through various forms of social control, from laws (macrolevel social control) to company policy (mesolevel) to peer pressure (microlevel). Each of these social norms is enforced through sanctions—consequences for violating the norms—that might range anywhere from being fired or scapegoated to imprisonment or death.

One way to think about activism is as an action that challenges social norms that are experienced as harmful or unfair. Where the change occurs depends upon where the action is directed. When social change efforts are directed primarily at the macrosociological level, one can expect initiatives focused on legislative reform, for example. Mesolevel social transformation is created by efforts to revitalize communities or make organizational policy more inclusive and equitable. Interventions at both the macro level and the meso level are widely recognized as activism. Typically, however, less attention is paid to how social change can be stimulated and sustained at the microsociological level of everyday person-to-person interactions.[9]

The smallest incidents of our social life contain all the moral and political values of society, all its structures of domination and power, all its mechanisms of oppression.[10]

—AUGUSTO BOAL

Shifting the focus of social change efforts to include the lived experience of ordinary people in the context of their everyday interactions can generate at least two important advantages. The first potential effect is a more widespread sense of agency and engagement—a much-needed tonic to counteract the pervasive disillusionment and perceived impotence that can stall progress toward positive social change. When activism is understood as something anyone can do, the perennial question "What can be done?" can be reframed as "What can I do?" Perhaps more significantly, the action is now focused on the intimate injustices playing out in the context of the present moment between people who are directly, mutually, and concretely affected by them. At the micro level, activism is no longer about political abstractions.

Microactivism engages and empowers every member of society to create meaningful social change in their own lives and affirms their capacity for leadership on the issues that matter to them. Everyone has a platform to do antioppression work and to participate in activism. The grocery store is a platform, the dinner table is a platform, and the staff meeting is a platform. Simultaneously, everyday microactivism redistributes the work of social justice into many hands rather than a designated few, making social change efforts more sustainable over the long term. Not only does a microsociological approach make activism more accessible, immediate, and sustainable; it also ensures that the impact is not limited to the grassroots micro level. As adrienne maree brown argues, "What we practice on the small scale sets the pattern for the whole system."[11]

It bears noting that a microsociological approach to systemic change such as the one described here should not be considered a replacement for working on other levels to make structural and ideological changes in social institutions such as education or health care, or as a substitute for legislative reform. Rather, microactivism works to support change in the relational fabric of our lives so that structural shifts correspond with authentic transformations in attitude and behavior, and so that inalienable rights and necessary responsibilities are experienced at the core of our beings and manifested in our everyday interactions with others.

What Is Embodied Activism?

The second advantage of focusing on the social microcosm as the locus of intervention stems precisely from the visceral immediacy of face-to-face interactions as the site of contested power and potential change. Although frequently overlooked as a source of knowledge and understanding, our embodied selves are critically important in the navigation of social power relations and the creation of new possibilities for being with one another.

There is increasing consensus that the lived experience of the body—that is, our bodily sensations, perceptions, and behaviors—plays an important role in how we experience the social world and how we enact unjust power relations. For example, years of cross-cultural research into nonverbal communication have established that:

- The meaning of our interpersonal communication is mostly conveyed nonverbally. Although we may take painstaking care in choosing our words in a challenging situation, most of the meaning of what we say to one another is actually conveyed through our postures, gestures, eye contact, and navigation of interpersonal space rather than through the words we speak.

- We are largely unaware of our nonverbal communication, and through it we unconsciously leak our implicit bias—both positive and negative—toward others. As a result, other people can often "read" our prejudices even when we have no intention of conveying them, and sometimes when we are not even aware those prejudices exist within us. Our unconscious bias can manifest in embodied microaggressions—seemingly insignificant nonverbal slights and insults directed at members of oppressed social groups that exact a damaging cumulative toll on the mental and physical well-being of those who endure them on an everyday basis.

- Our bodies help to create and maintain power differentials between members of different social groups by nonverbally signaling dominance/submission and inclusion/exclusion. These *asymmetrical interactions* occur when, for example, a member of a socially privileged group takes up more space, uses forceful and direct gestures, adopts an upright and expansive posture, and employs direct eye contact while simultaneously expecting those in subordinated groups to take up less space, lower their gaze, use indirect gestures, or take on a bowed posture.[12]

Considering the pervasive and nearly unavoidable nature of the examples above, it is not difficult to appreciate that the nonverbal component of social interaction may be the most common means of social control. Because so much of the damage we enact upon one another occurs on a body level, shifting the location of activism to include the microsociological dimension of social change necessarily means bringing the body into the mix.

Not only are our bodies a primary site for the reproduction of unjust social systems; they also bear the impact of discrimination and prejudice. Traumatologists are increasingly coming to understand the degree to which trauma (including the complex trauma of oppression) is experienced and held in the body—particularly in the nervous system—and expressed in our embodied relationships and interactions with others.[13] While our relationships are a primal source of human connection, oppressive social systems place a severe strain on those relationships.

At a fundamental level, oppression functions through disconnection—disengaging and separating us from others and from ourselves. And unlike other forms of trauma, the threat of relational rupture due to oppression is not in the past; it is still, and always, in the present. Research into the embodied experience of oppression has identified responses, patterns, and pain points in members of oppressed social groups that closely resemble the symptoms of trauma, including hypervigilance (senses on high alert, always scanning the environment for threats), disturbances in the autonomic nervous system ("revving" too high or too low), somatic dissociation (feeling disconnected from the body), and intrusive body memories (upsetting physical sensations without images or narrative).

If I can't dance, I don't want to be part of your revolution.

Although our bodies can be co-opted, hijacked, and colonized by the forces of domination and control, they are also crucial, and often untapped, sources of knowledge, creativity, and connection. The (mis)quote above, paraphrased from a statement by activist and scholar Emma Goldman, alludes to one of the central features of an everyday, embodied activism: the emphasis and insistence on pleasure and healing. If we are to meet the challenges of a sustainable grass-roots paradigm shift, our creative and generative impulses need to be enlisted and supported in our activism, not just our critical and destructive urges.

Fortunately, a wealth of emerging scholarship supports just such a stance. Derald Wing Sue, professor emeritus of psychology at Columbia University, has recently published the promising results of research into *microinterventions:* strategies for undoing, disarming, preventing, and resisting the harmful effects of micro-aggressions. Trauma models are increasingly focused on healing the embodied impact of oppression and on introducing strategies for cultivating resilience in and through the body.[14] Several neuroscientific studies suggest that interoception (the felt awareness of our body) is positively correlated with human empathy, and that both can be nurtured.[15] Strategies have been developed for enlisting our bodies in the effort to enhance our moral courage and resolve conflicts more effectively. In other words, the key ingredients for sustainable social change through embodied relational engagement are already available and waiting to be harnessed.

What Tools Do We Need?

Conventional approaches to activism would suggest that activists need two basic tools: analysis and action. For example, a women's rights activist needs the ability to examine and evaluate current events using a feminist/womanist interpretive framework. Any action they took as part of their activism would be informed by that perspective. When confronted with a particular social problem or challenge, they might ask "How is this sexist?" and "How are women being affected by this?" or "How is this issue created or exacerbated by a patriarchal social system?" The answers to these questions would then shape the activities undertaken to change the situation.

Although many activists use one primary lens through which to view the world—an antiracist lens, a feminist lens, a Marxist class analysis lens, or a critical disability lens, for example—seeing complex issues from only one perspective can sometimes cause activists to miss broader implications or overlook crucial viewpoints. For example, in the 1980s Black feminist activists argued that mainstream (read: White and middle class) feminists had largely ignored issues of racism and poverty and began to use the term *womanist* to denote this broader commitment to their communities.[16] In 1989, Black feminist legal scholar Kimberlé Crenshaw developed a theory to help explain the compounding of various forms of oppression faced by women of color. This concept of *intersectionality* has since been expanded to include multiple aspects of an individual's social identifications and locations. An intersectional analysis now typically includes considerations of class, gender, sexual orientation, ability, religion, age, ethnicity, immigration status, and other facets of one's lived experience within shifting social contexts. The ability to use multiple lenses to evaluate our experiences in the context of complex social worlds refines our understanding of what's going on and can help us direct our actions more effectively. But sometimes even the most insightful analysis of a problem does not lead to its resolution.

While analysis and action are powerful tools for social justice, they are essentially cognitive and behavioral in nature: we think about the problem and then act on it as if we were rational agents, unencumbered by our shadows. This cognitive behavioral paradigm has its roots in Western philosophical traditions and has been a dominant force in understanding human behavior for nearly a century. Anchored in a relatively simplistic cause-and-effect understanding of the world, a cognitive behavioral approach to change often overlooks the dynamic tensions, complex undercurrents, and tangled contradictions that emerge when the interpersonal and embodied dimensions of human experience are factored into the mix. In this book, you will hear from people whose activism is centered in the embodied and relational, and whose primary tools for social change might be more accurately described as *perceptiveness* and *responsiveness*.

Perceptiveness requires more than the use of multiple lenses and the incorporation of more than one perspective. It also calls us toward a vision for change that takes into account our hidden agendas and unconscious biases. Perceptiveness requires us to look inward as well as outward, and to recognize uncomfortable truths about our motivations, privileges, and priorities in doing justice work. Cultivating our perceptiveness necessarily means noticing how we use, misuse, and fail to use our power. Perceptiveness allows us to pick up the subtle but important differences, affinities, and power relations embedded in our everyday experiences. Engaging perceptiveness as a tool for change also invites us to pause and listen to the many voices of the body—how it wants to be touched and moved without being invaded or abandoned, when it needs to rest and breathe, and how it understands without words the pain we cause one another. Listening deeply to our body also invites us to listen more attentively to the bodies of others, recognizing that we are all members of each other.

While perceptiveness can support us in seeing and feeling the world around us with exquisite clarity and deep, visceral understanding, we are not spectators in our own lives. We are always engaged, always in relationship, always shaping and being shaped by the social contexts and physical environments in which we are embedded. Nor are we free agents whose actions have a linear causal impact on the world; rather, we are embedded participants in a network of relations, and our actions have a ripple effect. Everything we do (or fail to do) has an impact on others. Pairing perceptiveness with responsiveness completes the cycle of engagement with the world and fulfills the responsibility we have to ourselves and others to cocreate more equitable and enlivening processes, systems, and structures.

On a body level, responsiveness requires the cultivation of something that could be described as *somatic bandwidth*.[17] More complex and nuanced than a "window of tolerance,"[18] somatic bandwidth depends upon access to the lived, felt experience of our body as a necessary component in supporting a broad and flexible range of responses. It's not about taking the time to calm down or enlisting our prefrontal cortex to help us think our way through a problem. Rather, responsiveness means tapping into the deep and complex bodily sensations and impulses that are continually arising as we move through the world. It means learning how to give space to those sensations and impulses so we are informed by them but aren't necessarily driven by them. Responsiveness allows us the breathing space to generate interventions that are creative, not just destructive. Unlike reactivity, responsiveness opens us up to the possibility of disarming rather than attacking, enlisting rather than alienating, and it encourages the kind of inner alignment that allows us to embody integrity. When directed inward, responsiveness supports us in metabolizing our shame so it doesn't poison us, inspires us to anchor our rage in purpose, and allows us to navigate the complex dynamics of our own lived history of oppressive social systems with more grace. When directed outward, responsiveness supports compassion and courage in equal measure.

Cultivating perceptiveness and responsiveness as tools of embodied activism helps to shift entrenched patterns of relating to ourselves and one another so that new shapes, currents, dynamics, and energies can emerge in our actions and interactions. Sometimes these changes are nearly imperceptible—the slight lift of a chin or a quiet softening of the breath—and other times their manifestation is dramatic, such as refusing to surrender one's occupation of physical space to forces of authority. Together, perceptiveness and responsiveness can serve to bring our bodies into our activism in ways that help to *transform us* as we work to transform the world.

BODY STORY
Perceptiveness and Responsiveness in Relationship

At an international somatics conference a few years back, I found myself at a crowded evening reception following a talk I had just given. The topic of my session was controversial for some members of the audience, and I had fielded several challenging questions during the Q and A. I was feeling a little shaky but enlivened.

As I entered the ballroom where the reception was being held, I was immediately waved over to a corner of the room by two older men whom I recognized as senior teachers in the field. They immediately began peppering me with questions about my talk: Did I have any doubts about my perspective? Did I have research to support my claims? Had I considered the impact of my statements? As they spoke, they slowly began leaning in toward me, closing the space between us. Because they were both quite a bit taller, it felt like they were towering over me. Their gazes were intense and unwavering, their faces impassive. I felt the electricity of the charged dynamic course through my body. As I stayed with the sensation, it occurred to me that they were—probably unconsciously—signaling their dominance over me. As well-connected senior teachers, they were using their body language to underscore their right to interrogate me, a relative newcomer. *Aha!* I thought, and felt a small ripple of relief as comprehension dawned on me.

That embodied perceptiveness on my part then opened up an opportunity for responsiveness. I briefly felt through my options, noticing my embodied response as I imagined each possibility: I could puff up and make myself bigger, squaring my shoulders and jutting out my chin. I could back up and make myself smaller. I could stand there like a deer frozen in the headlights. I could soften my gestures and smile, making little apologetic motions with my hands. Fight, flight, freeze, appease. And in that moment, I knew that none of those responses felt right to me. They simply reinscribed old trauma patterns of dominance and submission, and I was tired of them. Besides, I actually liked these two men; they were interesting and deeply engaged with the topic at hand, even though the ways in which they were engaging with me seemed to be distorted by the privilege they held.

So instead, I listened to my body and let it take the lead in generating a new bodily response to the nonverbal dynamics among the three of us. Rather than bracing against the old "them against me" dynamic, I felt into the fresh and complicated "we"-ness of the moment. I leaned in, not away. And I beamed up at them. I took full, easy breaths and allowed my voice to deepen and strengthen. I released my shoulders. I allowed myself to move in a way that expressed the kind of engagement I wanted: empowered, comfortable, loving, free, and connected. And the two men responded immediately; their postures softened, they smiled more, one of them cracked a joke. Within moments, they had moved back to give me more space.

This example of perceptiveness and responsiveness is not a recipe. Not everyone would perceive the situation the same way I did, nor would they choose the same embodied response. That's not the point. The point is that when we tune into what's happening on a body level, the subtle and complex dynamics of our engagements with others become more apparent. And when we listen to our body's response to those dynamics, innovative creative impulses can emerge. We can shift old patterns and create new ones.

Of course, dismantling entrenched structures of persecution and inequity also requires that we identify what Lorde described as the "master's tools" so that our perceptions and responses don't inadvertently replicate the oppressive systems we are born into.[19] In the context of an embodied activism, I will argue that it is possible to notice what the master's tools *feel like* in our bodies (when we use them and when they're used against us). By the same token, we can also pay attention to how the tools of liberation land in our bodies. When we take time to notice our embodied responses to certain tools, we can begin to consider how we might develop a better feel for the tools we're using in our activism.

The following list offers a few examples of tactics often used in the service of oppression as well as some strategies that might better serve a process of mutual liberation and justice. As you read through the list, notice how you feel in response to each word. What sensations, memories, emotions, and impulses do they evoke?

SOME MASTER'S TOOLS	SOME DIFFERENT TOOLS
Violence (hostility, intimidation)	Peacemaking
Divisiveness (ostracism, scapegoating)	Inclusion and connection
Dishonesty (gaslighting, deception)	Honesty
Intolerance	Patience
Moral superiority	Humility
Secrecy and opacity	Transparency
Denigration	Respect
Competitiveness	Cooperation
Minimizing or inflating harm	Acknowledging harm and mistakes
Pity	Compassion
Shaming	Encouragement

Each interaction we have with others offers a new opportunity to choose how we respond, even when those interactions might feel despairingly familiar, loaded with innuendo and the memory of old hurts. When we're threatened or upset, which tools do we automatically reach for without considering the broader implications and long-term effects? Which tools do we need to intentionally cultivate and practice to be able to use easily and well? As we refine our responsiveness to challenging everyday situations, our perceptiveness also expands. We begin to see things we didn't see before—the complex nuances of an experience or inter-action we're having—simply because we're now able to respond differently.

What Steps Can We Take?

While perceptiveness and responsiveness can be thought of as broad, funda-mental capacities in embodied activism, there are also some practical steps we can take to bring the lived experience of the body into deeper alignment with how we navigate power in the context of our everyday lives.

1.   Explore oppression and privilege through our own body stories.

This book argues that doing the difficult work of examining how oppressive social systems have affected us on a personal level is one of the foundations of effective activism. When we don't fully appreciate how we've been wounded by patriarchy, racism, classism, heteronormativity, ableism, and other forms of discrimination, we're more likely to become triggered and reactive (rather than responsive) when these issues surface in our interactions with others. Exploring these old wounds and scars on a somatic level can be particularly transformative; although not all oppression is enacted through the direct subjugation of the body, our bodies are always on the line. This first step examines how we might listen to how our bodies respond to the everyday inequities and injustices we endure, and it begins piecing together a more coherent and compelling narrative—a story that doesn't simply examine the oppression we've encountered but one that also describes the impact of those oppressive experiences on our bodily sense of ourselves.

In the same way that our bodies are shaped by experiences of oppression, so too are they shaped by experiences of privilege. The unearned benefits of having a body that meets the physical criteria for membership in a socially dominant group are considerable. Even if we don't choose or want these privileges, they attach to us and afford us access and ease in countless ways: being able to walk down a city street without being afraid of harassment or attack, being able to gain access to public buildings using the main entrance, using the restroom that fits our gender, and not being seen as exotic, dangerous, or inferior just because of the way our body looks or moves. Each of us holds a unique combination of body privilege and bodily oppression, so unpacking the privilege our body affords us is as important a part of embodied activism as exploring the somatic implications of being oppressed. In developing this aspect of our body story, it can be particularly helpful to attend to social situations in which we feel particularly comfortable or unremarkable on a body level, considering that the luxury of inattentiveness can be a hallmark of privilege.

2.   Cultivate our senses.

Another key feature of oppressive social systems is a tendency to promote a dissociative or disconnected relationship with the felt sense of our body. While we are encouraged to identify with the outside appearance of our body, we are discouraged from feeling ourselves from the inside. Sensuality is often misappropriated as sexuality, and the palpable enjoyment of our own bodily capacities and appetites may be judged as self-indulgent or unseemly. The process of socialization in many cultures involves the cultivation of a master/servant attitude toward the body that views our physical senses as little more than tools in the project of self-mastery, rather than as dimensions of our humanity to be celebrated and enjoyed in their own right.

3.   Interrogate our nonverbal communication and liberate our movement.

As noted previously, research into the interpersonal dynamics of body language suggests that oppressive social systems are reproduced and reinforced by everyday nonverbal interactions with others whose social standing differs from ours. Learning how nonverbal communication informs and transforms our interactions with others can help us shift the patterns that reinforce harmful power dynamics.

Once we've explored how body movement can be co-opted by oppressive social systems to reinforce inequitable power dynamics, we can continue the process of liberation by experimenting with movement expressions that are unique to our own body. This might include allowing ourselves to stretch into new shapes, rhythms, and movement qualities that express who we are and how we feel on the inside. Or we might experiment with exploring relational space in new ways. Regardless of how we choose to play with movement to undo harmful patterns and create more liberated ones, this step focuses on claiming the pleasure and authority of our own movement preferences.

4. Reclaim our body image.

One of the most insidious ways that oppressive social systems maintain their power is by convincing the oppressed that there is something fundamentally wrong with our bodies. We are too fat, too flat-chested, too tall, or too short; our skin is too dark and our hair is too curly; we use a wheelchair or a cane; our eyes are the wrong shape or color. The list is endless, and the work of managing, correcting, and hiding what is "wrong" with us is exhausting and demoralizing. If we channeled all the time, energy, and resources devoted to making our bodies socially "acceptable" (to the degree that is even possible) and redirected it instead toward cultivating and celebrating the uniqueness of our body selves, the social world would be such a rich and vibrant place. This is not to suggest that we always find ourselves in a body that fits who we are, or that we shouldn't make changes to our bodily appearance. Rather, this book will argue that body shame is a tool of oppression and finding ways to reclaim our body image is a radical act.

5. Nurture an intercorporeal ethos.

Up until this point, it might seem as if embodied activism is a project undertaken by individuals whose agency and autonomy are unquestioned, in a context where the focus is on the development of our individual capacities and actions. However, nothing could be further from the truth. Understanding our own embodied history, cultivating our senses, interrogating our nonverbal behavior, liberating our movement, and reclaiming our body image are undertaken in the service of nurturing our ability to be with ourselves *and one another* in new ways.

The term *intercorporeality*, coined by philosopher Maurice Merleau-Ponty, emphasizes the role of social interaction in bodily experience. Not only are we always shaping and being shaped through our embodied interactions with others, the notion of intercorporeality argues that we are *members of one another* in a very physical and tangible way, not just in an abstract or idealized way. We depend upon the presence of other human and more-than-human bodies for our very survival, and we take aspects of those other bodies—for good and for ill—into our very deepest sense of ourselves as we develop, learn, and grow.[20] Even our flesh and bones are more porous and responsive to the environment than we often assume. Although we may sometimes feel like discrete and separate entities, being embodied is never an entirely personal affair.

We become who we are in the context of ongoing relationship with others, and we remain embedded and entangled in this intercorporeal field for the entirety of our lives.

Because of the inescapable mutuality of our bodily existence, a commitment to relationship is fundamental to embodied activism. For example, if we are members of one another, dividing our social world into "oppressors" and "oppressed" will not move us toward justice, because it fails to consider our own oppressiveness and others' humanity. Bringing together an intersectional analysis with an intercorporeal ethos means that each of us has some visceral understanding of how it feels to be disadvantaged as well as what it means to be privileged. If we reflect on these experiences deeply enough, we also come to realize that privilege does not necessarily make us happy (it simply makes us comfortable), and disadvantage does not sentence us to misery (it simply puts pain and fear in our path more often).

As we engage with one another around the social power dynamics baked into many of our relational interactions, it's crucial that we find some embodied empathy for one another. Every one of us has been thoughtless or insensitive at some point; we all have holes in our understanding and gaps in our knowledge. We all know the sting of injustice. There is no question that the systems and patterns of oppression must change, but the strategies to achieve change cannot include the vilification, abuse, or neglect of others unless we are prepared to feel the eventual consequences of that violence within our own flesh. In other words, an ethos of intercorporeality might be what Christianity's Golden Rule or the African philosophy of *ubuntu* feel like on a body level.[21]

At the same time, an intercorporeal ethos also means not taking in (or taking on) too much. In an era of constant exposure to information, it can be easy to be flooded with the compelling demands of disasters, crises, causes, and injustices around the world. While each of these events is legitimately deserving of care and attention, it's not possible for one body (or even one community) to respond to them all. Setting healthy boundaries and being committed to our own resilience doesn't just serve us; it ultimately benefits everyone we interact with. As we consider how to undertake a more embodied activism, staying intimately connected to our body can help ensure that we take the actions that matter most to us and have the most meaningful impact on the multiple spheres of influence we inhabit.

Overview of the Book

Drawing on the intersecting dimensions of somatics and social justice work, *Embodied Activism* articulates the importance of bringing the body into our individual efforts and collective movements. It offers a road map for exploring and transforming the political realities of our everyday experience by harnessing the felt experience of our bodies as the ground of our activism. From listening to our body language and questioning body-image norms to reconnecting with our sensual capacities, the book provides practical strategies for cultivating a visceral compassion for others and reclaiming a sense of everyday agency in the context of social conditions that might otherwise foster apathy, intolerance, and disconnection.

This book comprises seven chapters, each focused on a specific area where embodied activism has its roots or where its tendrils might reach. This introductory chapter articulates a rationale for reconsidering conventional approaches to activism and makes an argument for including the body in the social change work we undertake. The rest of the book takes up the foundational capacities required for an embodied approach to activism or describes a particular application for those capacities.

We begin with an exploration of how living in oppressive social systems shapes our bodies through what we learn from everyday experience. In "Our Body Stories," readers are offered a template for tracing the history of their own embodied experiences of oppression while also uncovering how the social privilege assigned to bodily features may have influenced their path through the world. Modeled on a form of embodied experiential inquiry, readers are encouraged to craft their own body story—in words, sounds, images, or movement—as a basis for a deeper personal knowing and as a creative springboard for collective transformation.

The third chapter, "Coming to Our Senses," argues for a revaluing of sensory awareness as a necessary counterpoint to the historical emphasis on intellectual argument in many social movements. The chapter begins by tracing the social and political roots of sensory numbing through an examination of *percepticide*, a term coined by Diana Taylor. Percepticide is the mechanism by which oppressive social forces require us to deny what we see, hear, feel, and know in the face of chronic and pervasive threat.[22] In this chapter, current sources and consequences of percepticide are identified across a wide range of social phenomena, from industrialization and colonization to addiction and apathy. The chapter then discusses how a return to our senses via the intentional cultivation of sensuality might serve as a potential corrective, noting how pleasure is often equated with irresponsible hedonism, while the hidden discipline of sensuality in creativity and meaning-making is overlooked. Given the philosophical and political legacy of antisensuality in many cultures, we might usefully consider sensuality as subversive. This chapter provides simple, everyday strategies for remembering our sensual selves as an essential tool for reimagining and reengaging with justice work.

The fourth chapter looks at how we might undo oppressive interpersonal relations by exploring—and potentially rewriting—our body language. Although our nonverbal communication conveys most of the meaning in our personal interactions with one another, we often pay more attention to the words we speak than to the body language that supports, elaborates, and (sometimes) contradicts our verbal message. Most of us don't really track what we're doing with our body when we're talking and have learned to disregard the internal cues that inform our body movements and facial expressions. Because most interactive nonverbal behavior seems to be enacted with little conscious awareness or choice, our body language can be a prime site for leaking implicit bias, reproducing unconscious and unfair power differences, and impairing rapport. In this chapter we explore how our nonverbal communication might be interrogated and rewritten so our interactions with one another can become more consciously respectful, authentic, powerful, compassionate, and fair.

In the fifth chapter we take up one of the most insidious and damaging ways that oppressive social systems enact damaging ideologies about bodily difference—through our body image. This chapter discusses a strategy for disrupting social norms of the body by working to disable the act of body norming itself. By turning toward the lived, felt experience of the body and intentionally cultivating the body's deep curiosity, we can access a subjective data set that informs and potentially transforms our relationship to objective body standards. In this way, the disruption of body norms becomes not just a strategy for resistance against oppression but also a process of creative, sensual inquiry that each body engages as an ongoing liberatory praxis.

The central premise of *Embodied Activism* is that our everyday embodied relationships are crucial sites for systemic change because the seemingly minor incidents of our social life are microcosms of larger oppressive structures, and because our capacities for kindness, respect, courage, and generosity are also manifested in and through these microinteractions. The sixth chapter of *Embodied Activism* recaps the strategies provided in earlier chapters—the cultivation of sensuality and the interrogation and transformation of body language and body image norms—and describes their application to the development of relational skills across a range of contexts. This chapter explores how we might consciously draw on our body's innate capacities for integrity and empathy as we navigate complex interpersonal terrain and negotiate unjust power dynamics. This chapter also extends the notion of relationship to include our engagement with what David Abram describes as the *more-than-human* world: the plants, animals, rivers, birds, and mountains that comprise our natural environment.

In the seventh and final chapter, we bring all these ideas and practices together into an integrative framework for embodied activism that is simple enough to use on an everyday basis yet powerful enough to make a real difference in how we live in our bodies and in the world. This chapter also offers recommendations for further exploration of embodied activism, including information on community resources, specialized training programs, and educational events. Although the exploration of how our bodies can become forces for change will be deeply personal, this work always necessarily occurs in the context of relationship and community. This chapter is intended to help readers get plugged into the networks, forums, and platforms that can help them thrive.

Engaging with the Text

Embodied Activism is offered as a road map of the intersection of two compelling territories: the deep and mysterious land of the body, with its primal currents of sensation and impulse, and the shifting, complex terrain of social change work. As a road map, it is designed to accompany readers on their own journey into how the political occupies the cells and patterns of our flesh and how our bodies are implicated in the process of transforming the world. While this book points out some landmarks and suggests some routes through these domains, each reader brings their own travel history, navigation skills, and preferred destinations. Each reader's journey also very much depends on their unique engagement with text: this is a book to be lived, not just read. To support readers on their journey, the book incorporates experiential exercises, reflection questions, and first-person narratives as catalysts in the process of generating meaning and creating knowledge.

Throughout this book, you will come across several "Body Story" sections, which present descriptive narratives drawn from the embodied experiences of people who have lived the issues being discussed in the text. While some body stories are my own, others are from colleagues, research participants, clients, and graduate students whose stories I have collected (with their generous permission) over the years. In each case, identifying details have been changed to protect their privacy. As you read these body stories, notice your own embodied response to them. You might experience a sense of affirmation or validation, perhaps manifesting in a deep sigh or a release of muscle tension. Alternately, you might feel irritated, agitated, or sad. Read the stories not as descriptions of universal truths, but as unique articulations of experience that you may or may not find some resonance with. Allow the points of resonance to illuminate some facet of your own experience, if that feels right. They have been written and offered for precisely this purpose.

"Embodied Praxis" exercises provide an opportunity for you to "try on" the material under discussion. The practices offered in these sections should be undertaken with thoughtful consideration of your own readiness and the appropriateness of the practice for your unique situation and context. As with the rest of the book's participatory components, these exercises are intended as springboards for exploration rather than as prescriptions for action. Adapt the exercises as you wish, omitting those elements that don't feel right in the moment, or doing just one piece at a time rather than the whole exercise. There is no right or wrong way to engage with the exercises, and no predetermined or expected outcome. As with the body stories, notice what resonates, where your curiosity is stirred, and where you might usefully draw connections between what you encounter in the exercise and what you experience in your everyday life.

"Embodied Reflection and Integration" sections offer opportunities for readers to engage in personal reflection on key questions related to the material being presented. As you sit with the questions, allow time for your body to respond to the inquiry, as it sometimes takes longer for sensation or intuition to bubble up than it does for our minds to provide an answer. Your response can take whatever form you'd like; it doesn't have to be in words. Maybe your answer arrives in images that need to be painted or drawn, or maybe the questions remind you of a song that needs to be sung aloud or some other impulse that needs to be acted upon. The form isn't as important as the embodied resonance it brings and the meaning and insight it invites. If you keep a personal journal, you might incorporate these reflection and integration responses into your journal entries.

This introductory chapter wraps up with an "Embodied Reflection and Integration" segment designed to provoke deeper inquiry into some of the reasons you may have picked up this book in the first place. Perhaps you've felt a sense of dissatisfaction or frustration with embodiment practices, trainings, or communities because of a perceived lack of awareness of the sociocultural and political dimensions of the work. Or perhaps you've been involved in activism in some form and have been disheartened by the toll the work took on your body and the bodies of your comrades and colleagues. Either way, the questions below are intended as prompts to assist you in clarifying your reasons for wanting to explore embodied activism and to bring your life experience into the mix.

EMBODIED REFLECTION AND INTEGRATION

- **Disembodied politics:** Reflect on any experiences of being engaged in social or environmental justice work and realizing that the body was missing for you. How did that impact your understanding of activism and the sustainability of the work? What was the impact on your bodily experience?

- **Depoliticized embodiment:** Reflect on any experiences of doing somatic/embodiment work (as a client, student, or practitioner) and realizing that it was missing a political dimension. How did the lack of a social power analysis and praxis affect your ability to explore, understand, and transform your embodied experience? Were you able to take what was valuable from the work despite the lack of critical consciousness?

2

Our Body Stories

How do I tell the story of my body?
How do I bring coherence and transparency
to random scraps of emotion, sensation, and impulse?
The wordless knowledge within my cells
remembers everything, analyzes nothing.
Is it possible to unravel the deeply knotted
strands of memory and meaning
that live in the muscles along my spine
flicker in the synapses at the base of my skull
linger in the touch receptors long after my brush with reality?
The stories of my body lie buried in my bones
waiting for the pull of muscle and sinew
and the tickle of a deep, deep breath
to float them to the surface of my skin.

In a return to what Indigenous cultures have long known and practiced, Western scholars in the arts and humanities are studying narrative structures to discern their role in making meaning of our lived experience. Educational psychologist Jerome Bruner suggests that there are two primary modes of thought: 1) narrative thinking, which is characterized by detailed, sequential, experience-based thought; and 2) paradigmatic thinking, in which the particulars are integrated into systematic categories.[1] According to Bruner, telling stories is one of the ways we come to know and understand ourselves. Making meaning of our lives is a process that occurs, in part, through the stories we tell about who we are.

Building on Bruner's work, Jean Clandinin and Michael Connelly argue that narrative offers a way to study lived experience and that social phenomena are a natural point of convergence for individual, collective, and cultural stories.[2] Because these stories are steeped in and emerge out of specific cultural norms and practices, they also shape group and individual identities. Narrative is a form of knowing that helps make sense of the human condition and a well-constructed story possesses a kind of truth that is real and immediate, allowing us to absorb deep meaning without detailed analysis. Stories are a primal form of creating and conveying meaning. Central to the body stories approach is the notion that the body is a crucial source of content as well as an ideal medium for communicating that content. To borrow from Brené Brown, who suggests that "stories are just data with a soul," crafting a body story may help us understand the soul of the body through how it shapes and has been shaped by the world.[3]

Given that stories function to communicate key aspects of socially constructed knowledge, we can think of *embodied narratives* as a particular kind of story—one that provides a means of shaping and relating the body's ways of knowing ourselves through the particular social contexts in which we live. If we listen carefully, our bodies can provide a depth and resonance to the stories we tell ourselves and others about who we are. Although bodily experience can never be fully captured in words or images—it's too layered, nuanced, and fluid—the body can be a powerful source of information and insight. At the same time, because the body is always changing, it resists and transgresses our attempts to make those narratives fixed, stable, or fully intelligible.

The language of the body is sensation, not words. As a result, it can sometimes be difficult to fully recall the experiences that might go into a body story, much less articulate them. Adding to the challenge is that one of the features of oppressive social systems is a tendency to repress or minimize the damage that results when power is used to dominate and control others. This relegation of oppressive interpersonal dynamics to the realm of the unconscious can occur for many reasons: an understandable desire to forget something that hurt us to help dull the pain it causes, a self-protective denial of the harmful impact of our privileged behavior on others, or a pervasive pattern of minimization (nothing to see here, folks!) that allows abusive social structures to continue to operate relatively unchallenged. At other times, the experiences of relational harm that are baked into oppressive societies can be so visceral and indelible that forgetting them is impossible. Visible or invisible, forgotten or ever-present, these experiences shape the subterranean landscape of our lives.

Even though embodied experiences of oppression can be elusive to capture or difficult to hold, creating a body story can take advantage of narrative's capacity to elicit unspoken knowing and provide a channel for authentic expression and communication. Writing (or drawing, or dancing) a body story taps into the body's ability to hold implicit memories and then helps to surface those memories and organize them in a meaningful way. And because each of us is the author of our own body story, we choose how and what to express in a voice that is uniquely our own. Our body stories weave together our beliefs, values, and personal realities in a way that preserves the integrity of our individual voice while tapping into the collective voices of our communities, cultures, and histories.

Although each body story is different, many of the body stories I have helped others to birth have focused on the body as the "abject other" in the larger story of their life. In other words, their body story tells the tale of how they came to dislike, fear, and mistrust their body as an inferior aspect of their self-identity. In these body stories, the central narrative describes a disowning of bodily sensations, needs, and desires in favor of abstract thoughts and external activities. The bodies in these narratives are often disciplined or neglected, and sometimes punished.

However, these body stories usually also have a counternarrative embedded within them: a story of how those same bodies resisted the pressure to disappear and insisted on being heard and felt. Sometimes this insistent presence takes the form of a health crisis, an injury or illness that drags us back into the body through pain. Other times, the body story is a love story, where the pleasure of sensation persuades us to fall back in love with our body, and by extension, with the bodies of others. Whether pain or pleasure, absence or presence, these narrative threads are inextricably woven together and exist within us in constant and subtle interplay. All of them can be understood as embodied responses to power, and like Michel Foucault's understanding of power as a network of relations, these narratives form a web of meaningful connections embedded within us and between us.

The purpose of writing a body story is to help us become more fully and consciously who we are, to practice getting at ourselves through our very cells and tissues. Initially, this is often a deeply experiential and introspective process. However, that doesn't necessarily mean that creating a body story is a solo project. Over many years of working with others to support them in a process of reclaiming the knowledge of their body, I have been struck by how revealing ourselves to other people can simultaneously make us more available to ourselves. Somehow, the conscious and intentional creation of our own embodied narrative in relation to the larger human story reclaims places within us that had been forgotten or abandoned and connects those places to the world. For this reason, I often recommend that some of the work of crafting a body story be undertaken with others, perhaps a close friend or therapist, or in the context of a learning community or affinity group. As philosopher Eugene Gendlin has argued, we are inherently relational creatures. Our bodies are shaped in the context of relationship, and it makes sense that the reshaping that can occur through creating a body story also belongs in shared space with others.

The guidelines for crafting a body story offered in this chapter are designed to help elicit certain dimensions of embodied experience that might not be immediately obvious or self-evident. Although the prompts may seem straightforward, creating a body story can be a complex and ongoing process. The experiential components draw deeply on established somatic work in experiential anatomy and sensory awareness, which in turn rest on Eastern and Indigenous traditions of illuminating embodied experience through reflection and expression. Both the catalyst questions and the experiential catalysts given work best when they are undertaken in a spirit of curiosity, self-compassion, and patience. The process of unearthing previous experiences of oppression often needs to be approached in layers, slowly and gradually, as if engaging in a process of somatic archeology. Take your time, pause for moments of reconsolidation and reflection, and ensure that you have the support in place, within and without, to do the work without causing further harm.

A Word about Trauma, Oppression, and the Body

Increasingly, oppression is being understood as a prolonged life stressor, and there is a growing body of research linking oppression and trauma. Rather than conceptualizing trauma as a single life-threatening incident, traumatology experts now recognize that a lifetime of experiencing prejudice, denigration, marginalization, and relational threat is also traumatizing, and it actually takes a bigger toll on the body and psyche. For example, a study that compared post-traumatic stress scores of people who had experienced single traumatic events with those of people who had experienced prolonged life stressors found that individuals with prolonged stressors reported more trauma symptoms than those who had experienced acute traumas.[4] There are now countless examples of members of oppressed groups who show full posttraumatic stress symptomatology in the absence of a single acute trauma. The evidence establishing a link between oppression and trauma has become so compelling that some trauma experts now define oppression as a collective trauma perpetrated between groups, existing on a continuum from microaggressions to macroaggressions.[5]

Many traumatologists also recognize trauma as a neurophysiological experience as well as a psychosocial one, and they agree that traumatic events have an impact on both the body and the mind.[6] Within the field of trauma research, the somatic effects of trauma have now been well documented, including neurobiological changes such as alterations in brainwave activity, size of brain structures, and functioning of processes such as memory and fear response, and psycho-physiological changes such as hyperarousal of the sympathetic nervous system, increased startle response, sleep disturbances, and increased neurohormonal changes that result in heightened stress and increased depression.[7]

It's important to recognize that the process of writing your body story may uncover or reactivate a trauma response. If you're currently struggling with emotional or psychological distress or if you know that your history around oppression is strongly charged, then working with someone who is trained in trauma work from an embodied social justice perspective will be helpful, if not essential. There's a list of resources at the end of this book that can help you locate someone to work with.

The body story that follows offers one example of how a history of trauma might show up in crafting the narrative of your own body. I interviewed Alex specifically for this book, and the body story that follows is a lightly edited transcript of that interview.[8] Alex tells their story in their own voice. If you'd like to read more examples of body stories, you can find them in my book *Embodied Social Justice.*

BODY STORY
Unwinding Trauma and Finding Strengths

I'm a beginning practitioner of somatic work. I'm training in Somatic Experiencing, NeuroAffective Touch, and Somatic Sex Education. I'm a bodyworker, and I also offer internal pelvic floor work. I've come to all of that through my own journey of trauma and my own understanding of my existence in late-stage capitalist worlds. I've done a lot of work around Whiteness and my own mixed-race family history. Half of my family is from colonizers, and the other side of my family were very colonized. It's so interesting how that racialization shows up in my body. Something that's now emerging in one of my practice specializations is working with predators, abusers, and people who hold the archetype of the colonizer. Because I've unwound both sides of this power dynamic in my own body, it emerges effortlessly in my work. Talking to other colleagues, they're like, "Oh, that is such a hard 'no' for me, working with those people." But not for me.

I was a full-service sex worker for three and a half years in my early twenties. It was a line of work that was deeply wired into me through the way my parents raised me, through a whole lot of different little things that I would call grooming. When I started sex work, there was this feeling of, "Oh my God, I am meant for this work." It was all choice on my part. It wasn't inherently traumatic, and it felt really empowering to step into a place where I was getting compensated for the emotional labor that I was already doing in intimate spaces. The hypersexuality was wired into me because of my family, so I was able to capitalize on it and become financially secure because of this thing that was wired into me. But as soon as I unraveled a couple of core pieces of my childhood trauma, any desire to do sex work just left my body—instant retirement.

I had been having a lot of meltdowns and a lot of relational problems in my personal life. I couldn't keep a relationship to save my life. I was also in overwhelm all the time, although I didn't have the language for that yet; I just knew that something wasn't right. I have a history of serious chronic health problems and medical trauma, and I've been estranged from my family for about a decade. So, my body was holding all these things. I eventually found a Somatic Experiencing practitioner who helped me unravel them, and I have been in remission for my chronic health issues for five years now. What was helpful with sex work is that because I had all these chronic health issues, I wasn't able to keep up with the built-in bodily demands of having a normal nine-to-five job. I simply couldn't show up. Sex work was a way to survive without having to run myself into the ground the way a nine-to-five would do.

It's been so interesting unpacking the hypersexuality thing. In my family line, there's so much sexual suppression, yet everything is also hypersexualized. Being a sex worker put me in the line of fire for all the stigma that comes with it. Sex workers are often scapegoats for people's sexual trauma in general. Suddenly, I was in a line of work that became an identity, even though it was just a job. I was thrust into this position where I was constantly doing emotional labor for strangers because of the projections and expectations they put on you about who you were. Even though I am retired and have unpacked all my hypersexuality, the amount of disdain I still get from cishetero White middle-class women is tenfold compared to what I get from men. I was shocked at the amount of violence that comes from women. Don't get me wrong; I've experienced my fair share of violence. But when it comes from female-identified people, there's a sense of deep betrayal. It's coming from a corner where it really hurts.

Although I've stopped doing full-service sex work, my work with Somatic Sex Education means I am still doing sex work, but in a different way. It's not dependent on me being hypersexual, but it's working with the sexual trauma that we all deal with. It's above the surface now. And I'm different inside compared to the way I was. It's a whole different approach. But for the past couple of years, I've been stepping into these very White-centric, colonial, capitalistic professional spaces. Just entering into these spaces being myself—mixed race and radical and coming from an "unprofessional" background—has been so hard. There isn't space for people like me. For example, in one somatic trauma training, I had to fight to be accepted into the program. They initially denied my application, and I came back with references behind me, insisting that they cannot withhold this work that is so necessary to people who need it. Even though I know inherently in my body what most of my clients will be dealing with, I'm spending most of the training fighting. It takes up so much bandwidth on my part.

I had an eating disorder for most of my life, from a really young age, that was imposed on me by my family and especially my mom. It went along with my chronic health issues, where everything I ate or anything I did made me feel bad. I was always in pain and always sick, so I decided, "I'm just not going to eat anything." Detoxing from my childhood trauma meant unwinding that eating disorder, so I now eat like normal person. Now that I'm eating enough for the first time in my entire life, I have a normal-sized, healthy body and a regulated nervous system. But I've also grown into a healthy human being.

I thought that now my body would stop being weaponized against me, but it still is, just in a different way. It has a lot to do with fatness and being a very curvy person naturally. When I was doing a buffer year between doing sex work and doing somatic work, I took a job with the federal government. All of a sudden, I was in this upper-middle-class White-centric capitalist structure. It was a shock to the system. And it was a very physical job. I would start every day in an office, but I wasn't sitting in an office all day; mostly I was out in a boat during the summer. And it was hot. One day I came into the office wearing normal shorts and a T-shirt. I was warned by management that I had to cover up and I wasn't allowed to wear what I was wearing. But my smaller, thinner coworkers who wore the exact same thing weren't ever told that. I hated that job so much. It was the most soul-sucking job, but I didn't have much of a choice. I was lucky. Most people in my position would have a hell of a time getting a decent nine-to-five job after a life of sex work.

In going back to that mixed-race place, as much as there has been conflict and wounding there, some really deep resources have also come forth; not just connecting to the qualities that my family has passed on, but this deep, energetic warmth that is unshakable. No one can take that away from me. One side of my family has a history of very strong and impactful women. So I have that going for me, and I often feel like there's some sort of luck that I have. I don't know what else to call it. Maybe it's magic, maybe it's luck. Maybe it's just seeing things in a certain way and finding creative openings.

I have a really strong constitution. My body is very physically strong, even if I do absolutely nothing to keep it that way. I can be sedentary for a year and a half and then jump right back into things. One of the things that I'm very grateful to my parents for is putting me in dance at a really young age and supporting me in having that skill. Dance has always been a place where I connect with my body in ways that nowhere else in the world supported. I know my internal world and my body and my physiology and my emotional body so well, and I attribute it to dance. Even though dance definitely encouraged my eating disorder, and a lot of the grooming I experienced was supported by dance culture, I've always been able to make it my own so that it wasn't a thing that victimized me or oppressed me. It supported a lot of really core things about me.

Now I'm at this place where I have all these great trainings under my belt. I have competency. I have confidence. I have the skills. But it has been impossible to find an office in this rental economy, and I cannot get professional liability insurance for my work. The only way I can somewhat legally practice my work is if I identify as a sex worker, and that doesn't fit. I'm doing trauma work. I'm doing bodywork. I'm doing scar-tissue remediation through manipulating soft tissues. I work with posttraumatic stress, developmental trauma, and sexual trauma. All these external barriers are constantly pushing down to the point where I'm afraid to do this work in public for fear of pushback. I've done all this training to get me where I am. I had to fight through the training because of all the different microaggressions and the lack of space for bodies like mine. Even finding supervision for myself has been difficult. I've been through so many awful consultations—people telling me I shouldn't be doing the work that I'm doing. I understand being cautious, and I understand being careful, and I understand encouraging containment of this work, because those things are super important. But it took me going through five or six consultants to get real support. Another example of the way my existence triggers people. The body is so political. God forbid anyone, including my clients, having autonomy over own their bodies.

I say this fully knowing that there are so many people in front of me that have been pushing that wall forward for me to even get to this point at all. People have been putting their bodies on the line so that I, as a past sex worker, could even survive up to this point. Their bodies have gone through so much. As much as I've been talking about the forward push, there is the back support of many decades and probably longer behind me.

As you read Alex's story, notice which elements of embodied oppression resonate for you. Do you connect with the parts of their narrative that speak about body size, illness, disordered eating, sexuality, or racialization? Consider if these are elements that you might want to include in your own body story. There are many examples of resistance, resilience, and microactivism in Alex's narrative as well. Notice your embodied response to those parts of Alex's body story and consider whether they might lead you to examples in your own life.

You can also use Alex's body story as a litmus test for your readiness to begin creating your own body story. How challenging, upsetting, or encouraging did it feel to read Alex's story, and what might this tell you about the emotional responses you can anticipate as you delve into your own narrative? As you can see from their story, Alex worked with a trauma specialist to help them unwind the trauma being held in their body, so consider what kinds of support might be necessary for you to do this work in a way that honors and respects what you and your body have been through.

Somatic First Aid Kit

Once you have the necessary support in place, you may still find a use for strategies to help you through any unexpected challenges in the process. Our bodies possess an extraordinary capacity for sensation, and inviting memories of embodied oppression can sometimes be experienced as upsetting, disorienting, or overwhelming. Although we cannot always predict where the inquiry into our embodied history will take us, we can usually take steps to respond to any distress that may accompany the discovery process. A "somatic first aid kit" is a set of skills that can help you in managing the emotional, physiological, and psychological responses to certain experiences. The following strategies may be helpful in dealing with challenging feelings that arise in the context of writing your body story. Try the ones that appeal to you and add your own strategies as well. There are many ways to move from a place of "too much" to a place of "just right."

Stop

Sometimes a sensation can be experienced as unsettling simply because it is unknown. Other times the feelings are inherently painful, or they evoke shame, anger, grief, or fear. Whatever the case, when something arises that feels too big or too deep to handle in the moment, the most sensible first strategy is to stop doing whatever is producing the sensations and attend to its impact. If you're writing when something comes up, stop and take a break, and do something else. Come back when you're feeling more settled or after you've had a chance to process what happened.

Ground

Alarm is a perfectly natural response to distress, regardless of the source. But when the source of the distress is in the past, grounding can help to counter our body's instinctive flight response so we can focus on resolving the discomfort. Grounding usually involves getting physically close and connected to the ground. For example, if you're standing, sit down; if you're already sitting, put both feet fully on the floor. Feel into your connection with the earth and notice its solid, ever-present support. Take a few slow, easy breaths, and with each breath, allow your body to gradually settle into gravity.

Orient

Orienting allows us to create some breathing space from an internal source of distress by deliberately focusing on the present-day external environment. Because the discomfort that arises while writing a body story will likely be something connected to the past, orienting to the environment also helps anchor us in the present. To orient yourself, use as many of the five senses as you have access to. For example, you might look slowly and intentionally around the room you're in. Name what you see (aloud if it helps), paying particular attention to things you find beautiful or comforting. Listen to the sounds inside and outside the room. Reach out to an object close by and notice its color, shape, and texture. If there are other people around, make physical contact (or eye contact) with someone who can provide a sense of safe connection. By emphasizing the perceptual reliability of the here-and-now setting, we reassure ourselves that our everyday world is still here despite our internal upset and disorientation.

Comfort/Connect

Once you've created some space from the upsetting feelings, offering yourself some comfort often helps to dissipate any remaining troubled energy. Find a place on your body where it might feel good to offer the physical touch of your own hand. This might be the place where the distress was experienced, or somewhere else that feels comforting to hold, such as your belly, chest, or feet. Take a few slow, easy breaths, and give yourself some words of comfort. Lean up against something solid, curl up in something soft, or wrap yourself in something warm (without losing your orientation to the external environment). Other people can also be a wonderful source of comfort if that feels right for you. Being able to talk about what you're experiencing can often help settle overwhelming feelings.

Bracket

Sometimes the upset we experience is tied to a bigger unresolved issue in our lives—something too large to digest or integrate easily. When this is the case, we can be torn between wanting to work on the issue and needing to take care of ourselves in the moment. Bracketing allows us to safely put aside our distressing feelings until we can address them more fully. The process of bracketing involves 1) acknowledging the feeling, 2) containing the feeling by placing it in your mind's eye behind a wall, in a box, or inside a bubble, and 3) putting the feeling aside for now with the promise that you will retrieve it when you are in a better position to address it. Keeping your promise to yourself to address the issue later is crucial to the long-term success of this strategy, so make sure the agreement is both specific and reasonable. Bracketing can also be useful when material emerges while creating your body story that relates to ongoing work you are addressing elsewhere, such as in therapy.

With these first aid strategies as part of your tool kit, writing your body story can become a journey that open ups new territories and perspectives without reinscribing old patterns of pain or distress. If you find that opening up to your embodied experience of oppression causes more problems than it resolves, however, it's important to reach out for help and support within your communities, from friends and family members, or from helping professionals who bring an awareness of social justice to their work. A list of community resources is provided at the end of the book.

Setting the Container and Choosing the Frame

While some folks prefer to jot down bits of memories and random insights on the fly, many body story writers benefit from creating an intentional time and space in which to engage in a process of deep reflection. While the techniques you use can vary widely, here are some aspects to consider in support of your process:

- Do I need peace and quiet to create, or am I more comfortable in a bustling cafe?
- Would I rather do these explorations alone or with someone else?

- How much time should I allocate for each body story session? Would it be helpful to set aside a set time each day or each week? Or would I rather write when the impulse strikes me?
- Would I be happier writing my body story on a computer, or do I need the tactile experience of paper and pen?
- When images arise in my exploration, how will I capture them?
- If movement impulses arise, how will I follow them? Am I going to want space to move in?
- How will I take care of myself during and after the creating process? Would it be useful to begin and end with a centering practice, make time for a walk, or arrange to have a conversation with someone after each writing session?

There are many ways to structure your body story. Some folks like to create a chronological sequence of events, while others prefer to focus on one issue at a time, such as body image. The choice of medium is also completely open; some people create a visual body map (more on that later in this chapter) or construct a collage, while others produce digital stories using video. You could interview yourself (or have someone else interview you) and then transcribe and edit the recording. You might write a poem or a play or create a dance. Regardless of how you go about it, remember that this story is yours, and the most important thing is that it's useful for you.

Some Catalyst Questions

I often recommend setting the groundwork of a body story by doing some straightforward reflective writing first.[9] Writing down memories that you can easily access (i.e., simply by asking yourself questions) can provide an overall sense of the known territory before moving forward with the experiential catalysts, which can surface material that is potentially less conscious and more unexpected. Here are just a few questions you can use as catalysts for your exploration:

- What are some of my experiences of oppression? What role has the physical appearance or functioning of my body played in these experiences?
- How do I relate those experiences to social categories of oppression? For example, do I understand them as experiences of racism, sexism,

ableism, or some other kind of oppression? Are the forms of oppression relatively easy to identify, or do some of the experiences intersect or overlap several categories?

- How have my experiences of oppression affected how I relate to my own body? This might include how connected I feel to my body, how I view my own body image, or the degree to which I am able to feel into or move certain areas of my body.
- How have my experiences of oppression affected how I believe others relate to or read my body?
- How have my experiences affected how I relate to or read the bodies of others?
- What role has nonverbal communication—for example, the navigation of personal space, or the use of gesture, touch, or eye contact—played in my experiences of oppression? For example, do I modify my nonverbal communication according to whether I feel oppressed in a particular situation? What have I observed in the nonverbal communication of others in these situations?
- What are some of the ways my body holds privilege?[10] How would I answer the above questions as they relate to my experiences of being a member of socially dominant groups?
- In what other ways has oppression had an impact on my body?

Many of these questions benefit from a reiterative process, i.e., writing a little bit the first time and then coming back to the question again after you've had some time to sleep on it and reflect further. In other words, your initial response to these questions may not be your full response. It can be helpful to give yourself time to ease into the questions slowly and allow the answers to unfold gradually.

Experiential Catalysts

Once you have an outline of the territory and some insight into how your body has been shaped by the oppressive forces in your social environment, you may wish to go a little further by engaging in some experiential somatic work. These experiential catalysts offer creative strategies for surfacing implicit memories, sensations, and insights that may otherwise be less accessible.

Focusing

One of the most useful approaches for accessing and integrating somatic experiences is a simple but profound technique called Focusing. Focusing is a self-directed process for attending to the body's felt sense of the experiences we've had and the various situations we live in. Developed by Eugene Gendlin at the University of Chicago in the early 1970s, Focusing was designed as a self-help tool to help illuminate and resolve a wide range of everyday concerns. It can also usefully be enlisted to help us deal with specific issues. Because of its capacity to engage our embodied implicit knowledge and bring it into dialogue with our explicit analysis of a situation, we can use it to unpack, deepen, and complexify how we hold our experiences of oppression.

The core of the technique consists of six steps that aim to establish an interaction between our rational understanding and our somatically rooted knowing. While many people can already draw on their body's implicit knowing without learning Focusing, these steps can be helpful for those needing a little extra help or structure to support them in gaining access to this inner wisdom. The description of the steps below is drawn from Gendlin's book, and I highly recommend reading the whole book before trying out the practice; it's short and easy to read, and many people use it as a reference for their Focusing practice.

EMBODIED PRAXIS
The Six Steps of Focusing

The steps listed below are the basic moves involved in Focusing. As you become more adept at the practice, you will naturally adapt, tailor, and clarify their use for your unique preferences. When trying them for the first time, go easily and gently. If something feels too difficult, you can stop or simply move to the next step. The Focusing steps are not a recipe, but rather a set of touchstones on a journey into yourself that you direct and guide.

1. **Clearing a space.** Take a moment to settle in, and then gently begin to pay attention inwardly, perhaps in your stomach or chest. Notice what you sense in your body when you ask "How is my life going? What is the main thing for me right now?" Allow the answers to emerge slowly. When

a response comes, simply notice it while allowing a little space between you and what has arisen.

2. **Felt sense.** As you sit quietly with what has arisen in response to the question you asked in step 1, allow one issue or concern to emerge that feels important to focus on. See if you can feel all the elements of this one concern without becoming immersed in them, keeping some space between you and what the problem feels like. Let yourself feel the unclear sense of the whole thing.

3. **Handle.** Get curious about the overall quality of this unclear felt sense. Allow a word, phrase, sensation, or image to arise from the felt sense itself. Take your time until something fits it just right. This word, phrase, sensation, or image is your handle.

4. **Resonating.** Going back and forth between the felt sense and the handle, notice if they resonate with each other. Notice if there is a little bodily signal that lets you know there is a fit—perhaps a sigh, a shiver, or a muscle release. Let the handle morph until it really captures the quality of the felt sense.

5. **Asking.** Now ask yourself, "What is it about this whole problem that makes it so [insert handle here]?" Return your attention to your body and be with the felt sense until you feel a shift, a slight "give," or a release.

6. **Receiving.** Be with what arises in a friendly, welcoming way. Appreciate your body for offering its wisdom. Even if you only experience a slight release in step 5, stay with it for a while before returning your attention to the world outside.

The only adaptation needed to use Focusing to illuminate a specific example of oppression is during step 1. When clearing a space, instead of asking the general questions "How is my life going? What is the main thing for me right now?" you can instead ask "What is the main thing for me right now about the experiences of oppression I've been writing and thinking about?" The words and images that arise during the Focusing process can become part of your body story, and the felt shifts you experience can help you hold the oppression you've experienced in a different, more resolved way.

In addition to using Focusing as a helpful tool in exploring individual experiences of oppression, some innovative work is being developed in the use of Focusing as a group-based technique to support our relational capacity in navigating power differences between members of diverse cultures and social groups. See my interview with some amazing psychology students in chapter 6 for more on how Focusing can support a more embodied sense of our connections across differences.

Movement Improvisation

If writing isn't your preferred medium for discovering and communicating somatic information, then maybe moving your body story will work better than writing it. There are lots of movement practices designed to help you access the kinesthetic dimensions of your life experience; Authentic Movement, Sensory Awareness, and movement improvisation are just a few examples. The spontaneous creation of movement without preset steps or predetermined structures means you're free to explore how your body wants to move in response to a question about your experiences of oppression.

If movement work is new to you, taking a class with an experienced facilitator is probably a good idea. There are some resources in the "Community Resources" section of chapter 7 that can provide ideas about where to learn more about somatic practices and movement improvisation before plunging in on your own. The interview with Christine Caldwell in chapter 4 also offers some insights into allowing our movement to emerge organically in service of decolonizing our bodies.

Images as Body Stories

One of the most powerful ways to tap into the material our bodies hold about living in oppressive social systems is through imagery. Especially when there are no words for what we have experienced, images provide a way to access, contain, and express the meaning of these events and how our body has responded to them. Whether these images are expressed through drawing, painting, collage, or sculpture, this nonverbal medium of communication offers a rich, nuanced, and immediately impactful way to convey our body story to ourselves and others.

Because imagery can be such a potent way to work with embodied experience, it's often a good idea to work with a facilitator if you're not already experienced in using this approach. Art therapists who bring a somatic, trauma-informed, social-justice-aware lens to their practice would be ideally positioned to facilitate a process of using images to craft your body story, but there are many others doing fine work in the context of psychosocial support with marginalized populations who have useful insights and practices to offer related to body imagery.

For example, a technique called body mapping has been used since 2002 in South Africa as a technique to support women living with HIV/AIDS and is being employed as a research methodology with undocumented workers in Canada.[11] Body mapping aims to support participants in recognizing and communicating the lived experience of their body, inside and out. Because the exercise involves interoception—how we feel inside our bodies—as well as body-image work, it becomes possible to create a map that documents both our life history of oppression and the lingering impact of these experiences. So a body map might include externally visible scars or injuries as well as internally perceived (but outwardly invisible) marks. Of course, a body map would be incomplete if we only documented the places where we have experienced pain, injury, or adversity. A body map can (and probably should) also illuminate those places where we hold strength, passion, and radical resistance.

Through the creative imagery elicited through body mapping, individuals can better see how their body is affected by their life world. As a somatic psychotherapist, I have worked with many clients in creating body maps. Each map offers a unique glimpse into the world of sensation, shape, color, texture, and symbolism contained within our bodies.

Making Meaning of Your Body Story

Engaging in the processes described above often results in a body story whose meanings and relevance are immediately clear; the words and images possess an inherent visceral resonance that requires no explanation or analysis. As the story emerges, it becomes obvious how these experiences shape your current reality and even how you might reshape how they live within you, perhaps by making an inner bodily shift or by taking action in the world. In other words, writing your body story often leads directly to discernible changes in how you relate to your body and the bodies of others. Sometimes, however, the meaning of the experiences that emerge through creating your body story are not so clear. When this occurs, it can be helpful to engage in a process of reflection and distillation to help the significance of your body story emerge more fully.

For this process, I often draw on the work of experiential educator David Kolb and colleagues. In his observations of how people learn from experience, Kolb postulates a natural cycle of learning that includes reflecting on the experience, distilling those reflections into concepts, and experimenting with new behavior based on what was learned from the experience. I've adapted Kolb's cycle specifically for use in working with the embodied experiences of oppression, in a cycle I call the Cycle of Embodied Critical Learning and Transformation (you can read more about this model in my book *Embodied Social Justice*). For the purposes of this chapter, here are a few aspects of the cycle that can support making deeper, fuller meaning of your body story.

The *embodied critical reflection* phase can be very useful in surfacing the richness of an experience when it initially feels too much like a recitation of facts—for example, if there is a passage in your body story that is factually accurate but reads as if it happened to someone else. Sometimes this distancing from our own experience serves an emotionally protective function, so it's important not to push too hard or too quickly to close that distance. The desire to reflect on an experience usually occurs naturally as soon as we're ready to safely learn from it, so if your strong impulse is to push the experience away and not look at or think about it, then you might want to wait to work with a counselor, spiritual advisor, or other skilled professional before trying to unpack it further.

In fact, one of the best ways to engage in reflection is to talk things over with someone else. If you've ever had an upsetting experience and then immediately wanted nothing more than to hash it out with a trusted friend, that's the natural impulse to engage in reflection. Reflection allows us to mull things over, to hear ourselves think aloud about what happened, and to gain some perspective on the experience by bouncing it off someone else who has our best interests at heart. Even if your preference is to *not* talk about a troubling experience, you might well find yourself reviewing it over and over on your own, turning it this way and that, in an effort to make better sense of it.

Again, this natural process of reflection is something most of us automatically engage in when wanting to learn from our experience. However, sometimes elements get left out of our reflections due to a process of socialization that dismisses the body and discourages a critical analysis of power. One way to counter the effects of this socialization is to intentionally add embodiment and power dynamics back into the practice of reflection. You can incorporate these elements by asking yourself a few simple questions:

- Do I have enough support, time, and care to listen to my body and respond to what it's telling me? Would it be helpful to slow down the process, so my body has a chance to weigh in? What does my body need in this process?

- Am I aware of any bodily sensations, movement impulses, or images as I reflect on this experience? What nonverbal communication was occurring during this experience, and what meaning did I make of this nonverbal information?

- As I reflect on this experience, what's my sense of where power was held? Was it held by a single person? By an administrative or institutional procedure? By multiple people? How did these power dynamics shape what happened and how it landed for me?

- How does my experience connect with the experiences of others who are oppressed? How does my body story resemble (or differ from) the stories of people with similar social identifications or locations? What might I learn from them?

By allowing ourselves to reflect, patiently and compassionately, on what has happened to us in an inequitable and unjust world, it becomes possible to deconstruct, problematize, and eventually transform our embodied experience of oppression. Engaging in reflective processes that include somatic and social data allows us to generate critical insights that are embodied as well as cognitive, to privilege self-generated insights over those generated by others, to name the unnamed and unnamable, and to make space for an embodied, felt shift toward a new way of being in the world.

Sharing Your Body Story

Once your body story is in a place where you feel ready to share it with others, consider how you might want to communicate it, and with whom. If you're undertaking the creation of your body story as part of a group, you might simply share it with other members of the group. If you're working with a therapist or another facilitator, perhaps you share it with them and a few chosen others—maybe some close friends or family members. You might also decide not to reveal your body story to anyone, instead considering it a document of your own personal journey that works best when you keep it private.

Regardless of who you share it with, it's important to protect your body story from inadvertent appropriation and unhelpful analysis from others. To help prevent others from responding to your body story in ways that don't feel good, you can specify how (or even if) you'd like feedback from them. Consider what you're hoping for from others—affirmation? Supportive witnessing? Constructive questions? Insightful analysis? Possible connections to their own experience?—and then ask for that. Be sure to also specify whether they are welcome to discuss your body story with others, or if you would prefer that they keep the material you've shared confidential.

Sometimes it can even be affirming to share our body story with strangers. For example, for the past decade or so, I've been working with research participants and graduate students to create spoken-word and movement performances based on the body stories of those who have experienced oppression and injustice across a range of social identifications. In these performances, actors and dancers present the actual words of a research participant's body story, which are then crafted into a series of dramatic passages interspersed with music and movement. Although it can feel a little scary to place one's body story in the hands of others and then see it performed in front of an audience, the experience can also offer a kind of visceral acknowledgement of one's own struggles and accomplishments. In the words of a research participant whose body story was presented in one such community performance:

I had this experience of being validated and witnessed in a very unself-conscious way. There was this sense of my story being heard. I thought, "Ah, now this whole room understands my experience." I think about how maybe a member of the audience has never had that particular experience—never had to think about it because of their own privilege—but when they see the performance, they get not just the fact of it, but some of the emotional impact of it, how it feels in the body to feel unsafe and exposed. There is an added layer of safety when my body story is performed by someone else. My experience is communicated, but I do not have to worry about how others respond to my story. It is as if the performer is a buffer between the person whose story it is and the people who hear the story. There's this little bit of space in between to digest, to think, and to feel.[12]

You can read more about this approach to embodied social justice research in my chapter on body stories in *The Art and Science of Embodied Research Design* (cited in the note above).

Through crafting our own body story, it becomes possible to develop a better sense of how our bodies have been affected by the sociocultural contexts in which we live. We come to understand that some of what we had considered an inherent quality of our bodily makeup actually originated from outside ourselves, in the cultural and social milieus in which we are embedded. Through sharing our body stories, we come to know that some of the pain and difficulty we struggle with is not uniquely ours; we share it with other human bodies across a wide spectrum of identity and experience. This foundational knowing can, in turn, support embodied strategies for resistance and resilience-building that shape how we engage in activism and how we understand our unique role in changing the world. Some of those strategies are presented in the chapters that follow.

3

Coming to Our Senses

The political lives within our very tissues and movements.

—MARY WATKINS

Percepticide is a term used to describe the mechanism through which oppressive social forces require us to deny the truth of our senses in the face of chronic or pervasive threat. In order to survive unbearable conditions, we replace our sensory experience with a false or dulled perception—an act of simultaneous self-protection and self-harming in which our sense of what is happening around us is internally silenced or disavowed. Although Diana Taylor coined this term in reference to public spectacles of violence so horrific that they forced the public to look away, the notion of percepticide can help us understand our response to the more subtle, indirect threats of persecution and exile that many of us encounter on an everyday basis. Living in a world in which we are repeatedly reminded of our precarious safety and belonging, it is sometimes necessary to know nothing, hear nothing, and see nothing simply to get through the day. Over time, we may find ourselves unable to trust or even access the full range of our sensory capacities.

In this chapter, some current sources and consequences of percepticide are identified across a wide range of social phenomena, from industrialization and colonization to addiction and cultural trauma. This chapter then discusses how a return to our senses through the intentional cultivation of sensuality might serve as a medicine for some of the harm that percepticide inflicts. Beyond the specific impact of percepticide, it's important to note the broader philosophical and political legacies that encourage bodily constraint and deprivation as moral imperatives. In many cultures, physical pleasure is equated with sinful self-indulgence in a way that overlooks the role that sensuality plays in everyday creativity, learning, and meaning-making. Given these relics of somatophobic indoctrination, we might usefully consider sensuality as subversive. The following pages provide some simple everyday strategies for remembering our sensual selves as an essential tool for reimagining and reengaging social justice work. But first, a little context is in order.

The Legacy of (Dis)Embodiment

To fully engage in the project of reclaiming and engaging our sensory capacities in working toward liberation and justice, it's necessary to understand how many of us in modern Western societies came to lose touch with our sensuality in the first place. Developmentally, the loss of uninhibited sensory engagement with the world often occurs through child-rearing practices that focus on self-control of the body. Although learning how to walk, talk, read, and write requires the development of a range of sensorimotor skills, the way in which this learning occurs often emphasizes repetition and discipline rather than play and discovery. As we get older, many of us encounter the restrictive and regimented social norms imposed during our schooling—sitting quietly, inhibiting movement, listening to the teacher, and keeping our eyes on our work. While neurodivergence or early childhood trauma may complexify this socialization process, few of us escape our upbringing without experiencing a forced disconnect between body and mind and a corresponding loss of sensory richness and freedom.

Historically, it is possible to trace a similar path from bodymind unity and sensory integration to disembodied compartmentalization. Most Indigenous cultures understand their worlds holistically, and this integrative perspective is reflected in ancient conceptions of the body/mind/environment relationship. For example, many primal cosmologies recognize the natural elements of earth, water, air, and fire as the essential components of life. In these cosmologies, everything is composed of these elements, including the human body. By viewing the human body as intrinsically embedded in the larger world through its elemental composition, and by viewing these elements as informing both our physical and psychological constitutions, these Indigenous perspectives understand the body/mind/environment relationship as essentially unified, and the bodymind as a unified microcosm of the larger universe.

Although some Eastern philosophies include practices that may appear to strive toward transcendence of the body through self-discipline, bodymind unity is also an ancient Eastern philosophical concept. Philosopher and embodiment scholar Yasuo Yuasa argues that that transcending the self/ego is not the same as transcending the body and asserts that early Taoist and Buddhist precepts understand the bodymind as an evolving system that can be developed through practice and attention.[1] According to Yuasa, all knowledge must be cultivated—that is, learned through the body—and the lived experience of the bodymind unity is the methodological route to enlightenment.

In contrast to Indigenous and Eastern conceptions of the bodymind, the Western intellectual tradition has historically separated body and mind, devaluing the body and its perceptions as unreliable and illusory. In a philosophical legacy extending from Plato and Socrates through to Descartes, the physical senses are regarded as imperfect instruments in perceiving the objective truth of external reality. Only the mind is considered capable of accurately discerning and understanding the true essence of existence. In fact, bodily experience is thought to inhibit and impair our attempts to understand the true nature of reality. This perspective has been profoundly influential on the Judeo-Christian theological tradition as well as later philosophical schools of thought. In many ways, Western philosophy has been dealing with the implications of mind/body dualism posited by these early Greek philosophers since it was initially proposed.

While this distinction between mind and body can be traced to the Greeks, French philosopher René Descartes provided the first systematic account of the mind/body relationship in the Western philosophical tradition. In his treatise *De homine,* Descartes provided the first articulation of a mind/body interactionism that argued that conscious sensation was an example of body affecting mind, and voluntary action came about by mind affecting body. In either case, body and mind were conceived as separate entities, and body was considered distinctly inferior, closer to animals than to humans.

Considering that Descartes was writing at the time of the European Enlightenment, when human potential was being rediscovered and celebrated in the

West, his emphasis on the potential of the rational, cognitive aspects of human experience was to have a lasting impact on the subsequent devaluing of the body and would govern most subsequent Western philosophical thought until the late nineteenth and early twentieth centuries. Allan Johnson describes the impact of this legacy on embodied experience: "Many men live as though the body and its needs are repugnant . . . as though the body were merely a machine, as though a life that denies or even punishes the body is superior to a fully embodied life. Nature, the body, and women become the 'other,' objects of repressed desire and longing as well as fear."[2]

Phenomenology offers perhaps the most significant modern philosophical challenge to Cartesian dualism's approach to the body. Developed in Europe in the first half of the twentieth century, phenomenology is literally the study of "phenomena" from a subjective perspective—things and events as we experience them from a first-person point of view. By extension, phenomenology is also interested in the study of consciousness and how we make meaning of experience.

Maurice Merleau-Ponty's work offers an embodied, existential form of phenomenology that emphasizes the role of the body in human experience and attempts to resist the traditional Cartesian separation of mind and body. In *Phenomenology of Perception,* Merleau-Ponty offers the concept of the "body-subject" as an alternative to Descartes' *cogito* or thinking self. He argues that consciousness, the world, and the human body are intricately intertwined and mutually engaged, and that physical reality is not composed of the unchanging objects of the natural sciences but is instead a correlate of our body and its sensory functions. He asserts that "my existence as subjectivity (i.e., consciousness) is one with my existence as a body and with the existence of the world."[3] In essence, Merleau-Ponty argues that consciousness is always embodied, and the body is infused with consciousness of itself and of the world. The implication of this assertion is that one's own body is not merely a physical object but is rather a necessary condition of experience—a perspective that aligns with earlier Indigenous understandings of the mind/body/environment relationship.

Merleau-Ponty's elaborations of body image and embodied intersubjectivity also provide key concepts in understanding a phenomenology of the body. Our *body image* is the corporeal schema or map that unconsciously structures our perceptions, movements, gestures, posture, and sense of position in relation to the environment; in short, it accounts for our way of being in and through the body. For Merleau-Ponty, this body image is a work in progress; it develops through experience in much the same way that a photographic image gains definition and resolution as it develops. Like the Eastern perspectives articulated earlier, Merleau-Ponty argues that the strength and clarity of the mind/body/environment relationship is not a given; rather, it needs to be cultivated through embodied praxis.[4] This concept of body image posits that the body is central to everyday experience, and it suggests that the body is in a constant state of becoming.

Although the notion of body image provides a fertile ground for exploring the embodied aspects of subjectivity and intersubjectivity, phenomenologists have tended to neglect the social and historical implications of these ideas. However, critical embodiment scholars are increasingly emphasizing the social and historical contexts of body image to suggest that because the body is central to experience, it is also central to social identity—and because the body is always in a process of becoming, it is also open to transformative social contexts.

Many are also noting how embodiment has been characterized by polarized binaries—male/female, healthy/ill, heterosexual/homosexual, Black/White—and how the association of the body with gross, unthinking physicality extends to negative associations with subordinated social groups, such as women, people of color, and the disabled.[5] The oppressed are identified and definitively assigned to social groups based on their bodily characteristics (e.g., skin color, size, physical features, bodily capacities) and are simultaneously treated as if they were just bodies without minds, hearts, or souls.

Because the body features so prominently in the articulation of social difference, it is a significant basis for social oppression as well as a crucial site for resistance. Understanding how the body is increasingly regarded as a site of personal identity, how our social status is reflected in our relationship with our body and the body language(s) we speak, and the crucial role society plays in our notions of the body are all necessary foundations for exploring the politics of embodiment and how an embodied activism can offer a radical shift in how we go about engaging in social transformation. Considering that one of the most damaging consequences of oppressive social systems is violent disconnection—from ourselves and each other—then it follows that healing those rifts must also begin with the body.

Reclaiming Our Sensual Selves

*Embodied awareness is the way back home—intimacy with where and how
we are right now, with what is happening and how we are meeting it. My
intention is to lead you into the heart of your life. Inside your body, where
everything happens—within a quality of listening rather than knowledge,
of feeling rather than reaction.*[6]

—MARTIN AYLWARD

Thomas Hanna, founder of the field of somatics in the United States, defines the
soma (after the Greek word meaning "living body") as the body as experienced
from within. A somatic perspective represents a significant departure from conventional ways of thinking about the body and reality. Drawing on existential,
evolutionary, and phenomenological perspectives, it suggests that we don't just
perceive reality through our bodily senses; reality is *constructed* by the way in
which we perceive it. This reality construct requires both sensory and cognitive
perception. On this view, body and mind are not seen as separately functioning
entities but are connected through the integrative function of perception that
relates us to our environment. Somatic theory suggests that what we experience
as reality depends on the quality of somatic perception we bring to our engagement with the world. Rather than detracting from the truth of our reality, the
sensory perceptions of our bodily experience are essential to any inquiry into
the nature of reality, including social reality.

As our sensory and cognitive perceptions create an integrated somatic
experience of our external environment, body and mind also work together to
help weave the perceptual fabric of our internal environment. This inner world
includes awareness of our internal biological functioning as well as our psychological reality—ideas, emotions, imagination, and beliefs. The mind is not seen
as a separate system with distinct components and self-contained dynamics.
Rather, it is one of many facets of somatic experience. Further, what are typically conceptualized as "internal" processes—human awareness and biological
function—are understood as integrally connected with what is understood as
the "external" environment. From a subjective, first-person consciousness, reality is located in the inner realm while being simultaneously connected to the
external world. Or, more accurately, reality is an integrated cyclical process in

which perceptions inform responses, which affect environment, which shapes perceptions, and so on.

This idea is important to understanding how somatic experience impacts social reality. In Western culture, we are not accustomed to expecting changes in our social environment as a result of changes in our bodily environment, especially when those changes may only consist of a shift in somatic awareness, rather than a change in overt behavior. A somatic perspective understands that a change in one aspect of our experience affects all the other aspects. Our perceptions of the external environment affect our perceptions of the inner one. Shifts in physical musculature create adjustments in our emotional state. Changes in sensory phenomena inform changes in cognitive perceptions that, in turn, affect our relationship to the environment. And, ultimately, our engagement with the environment both forms and informs reality.

When we are socialized to dominate or ignore the body, this natural cycle begins to get unbalanced. A somatic perspective understands one of the implications of this imbalance as a narrowing or constriction of consciousness that results in less freedom, fewer choices, and less effective patterns of embodied engagement with the environment. Somatic practices are designed to help restore our capacities for engaging with our world by facilitating an awareness of how we use and live in our bodies. Reclaiming our bodily awareness allows us to begin to shift old patterns of engagement with the environment, including those entrenched by oppressive social systems.

Thomas Hanna's foundational text on somatics, *Bodies in Revolt,* clearly articulates his argument that the need for a return to the experiencing body is related to the evolution of the human species, in direct response to industrialization, rationalization, and the commodification of the body. This somatic view of the body as key to personal and social transformation has now been taken up by countless others. In *My Grandmother's Hands,* Resmaa Menakem articulates how racial trauma is passed down through generations and offers strategies for engaging the felt experience of the body to transform the collective pain and disconnection caused by racism. In *In the Realm of Hungry Ghosts,* physician Gabor Maté describes how addiction begins as a fundamental human need for connection, and he delineates the closely interrelated somatic, psychological, and social dimensions of addictive impulses. Staci K. Haines, in her book *The Politics of Trauma,* invites readers to examine the social, political, and economic roots of personal and collective trauma and articulates how racism, environmental destruction, sexism, and poverty are rooted in a criminal disregard for the bodies of others. Shared among these authors and many others is the notion that reclaiming our bodies is both a personal and a political act.

So how do we go about this reclamation? What is this bodily sense of ourselves? Beyond the classic five senses, what other sensory inputs contribute to the ever-changing gestalt of sensations that lets us know we're alive? The science of our senses is still developing, especially in terms of new research in neuroscience, but the three domains described in the following pages offer a basic road map through the territory.[7]

Interoception: Sensing Within

Often described as our *sixth sense,* interoception refers to the sensory information arising from within the body. (In contrast, exteroception refers to the information that comes to us from *outside* our bodies.) This internal flow of data includes sensations of pain, pressure, temperature, sexual arousal, fatigue, hunger, and thirst—information designed to let us know when critical body functions are out of balance or need attention. By letting us know when we need food, water, warmth, and other life necessities, interoception helps to keep us physically safe and healthy.

Interoception is also likely the basis of our emotional life, particularly when we think of emotions as consisting of varying degrees and shades of comfortable/uncomfortable. There is increasing research evidence that the neural substrates responsible for the subjective awareness of emotions are based on physiological states.[8] Interoception also seems to serve as the foundation for our subjective sense of ourselves as a feeling entity. In other words, interoception provides the underpinning for our overall sense of self.

However, we all vary in the degree to which interoceptive signals reach our conscious awareness. These variations are either a function of natural neurodiversity—we're all wired a little differently—or are due to traumatic experiences that disrupt how our autonomic nervous system handles information. For some, interoceptive signals are quite muted. For others, the sensations arising from within can be so intense that they are overwhelming and exhausting. Whether our body speaks to us loudly or softly, the key to harnessing our interoceptive awareness seems to lie in our ability to modulate and make sense of the information that our bodies are sending. In a way, cultivating our interoceptive awareness can be thought of as a particular type of inner listening that's both sensitive enough to capture the subtle whispers and consistent enough so the body learns it doesn't need to shout to get our attention. Over time, we learn how to adjust the volume so we can hear and understand what our body is trying to tell us, even when the message is complex and nuanced.

The intentional, focused, and compassionate witnessing of these inner body sensations is foundational to the development of somatic literacy (knowing who we are in our bodies) and somatic bandwidth (having a range of capacity for feelings and sensations).[9] Many somatic practices focus on the exploration and cultivation of interoception and can offer useful pathways to enhance our sense of ourselves through our inner body sensations. If you're not sure how much interoceptive awareness you currently have, there are now reliable assessment measures that can help give you a baseline reading. The Multidimensional Assessment of Interoceptive Awareness is one such tool, and the second version (MAIA-II) is free and widely available.[10] Once you have a basic understanding of where your interoceptive awareness might need muting or brightening, there are a range of practices that can help you fine-tune your reception of these essential bodily signals.

The Focusing practice described in the last chapter can help cultivate your ability to listen to your body, as the *felt sense* might be considered a form of interoception. Many mindfulness practices, especially those that focus on breath or body scanning, can also be powerful interoceptive awareness tools. There is also some evidence to suggest that somatic exercises that work to strengthen the vagus nerve can be helpful in enhancing interoception.[11] In *Discovering the Body's Wisdom,* Mirka Knaster offers brief introductions to over fifty somatic practices that help to hone interoceptive awareness, among other things.[12] The book also provides illustrations, exercises, and practitioner biographies, so it's a great introduction for those who are just beginning to delve into sensory awareness work.

So what does interoceptive awareness have to do with the practice of social justice? Because embodied activism is always also a relational practice, being able to be with our complex, messy, and sometimes painful bodily sensations also helps us to *be with others* (and all their complex, messy, and sometimes painful feelings) in the face of injustice. Especially when tempers flare or misunderstandings arise, being able to be fully with ourselves without abandoning the other (and conversely, being fully present for another without forsaking ourselves) helps us stay in the good trouble that leads to greater understanding across difference and more resilient, honest relationships. We'll discuss this topic more in chapter 6, "Activism in Embodied Relationship."

EMBODIED PRAXIS
Listening Within

Find a quiet place away from everyday distractions where you can spend a couple of minutes tuning in to the sensations arising from within your body. Sitting or lying comfortably with eyes closed or softly open, allow your awareness to center on your breathing. You don't need to take slow or deep breaths; just find a way to breathe that's comfortable and easy.

As you notice the sensations of breathing—the expansion of your lungs, the sensation of air passing through your nostrils, and the slight fanning movements of your rib cage—see if you can also notice other bodily sensations. Are you aware of feeling any hunger? If you've recently eaten a meal, can you feel the fullness in your belly? What about temperature? Are there places in your body that feel warm or cool? Can you feel the weight of your body pressing against the floor or the chair? Spend a few minutes hanging out with the various sensations arising from your body. Just notice what's there without necessarily trying to change or fix it. Then, after a couple of moments, allow your attention to shift back to the world around you. Take a nice, easy breath and maybe a stretch or a yawn to help bring your focus all the way back.

Don't overdo it—even thirty seconds is fine to start—and then add more time and more dimensions of interoception as you progress. If you encounter uncomfortable feelings, remember the guidelines in the somatic first aid kit in chapter 2. Although there can be some benefit to making room for discomfort as a way to stretch your capacities, overall the practice of cultivating interoceptive awareness should be pleasurable. Play with the practice so it becomes second nature to tune into what your body is feeling as you move through your day and through the world. Once you have a handle on checking in with your interoceptive awareness on a regular basis, you can broaden and deepen your capacities by exploring some of the somatic modalities presented in the "Community Resources" section in chapter 7.

Proprioception: Sensing Movement

It has been said that revolution begins in the muscles. In other words, the impulse to resist, disrupt, and transform the world in which we live arises not just from our beliefs and values but also from our flesh. This notion is central to an embodied activism. The functional unity of the body/mind/environment system means that our thoughts and feelings shape our nerves and tissues, which in turn shape our worlds.

Nowhere is this deep interconnection more strongly felt than in our instinctive desire to move—to stand up, push back, hold on, and reach out. On a body level, our awareness of these movement impulses and actions is called *proprioception*. Proprioception can be defined as the perception of the relative position of neighboring parts of the body and of the strength of effort being employed in movement. In humans, it is provided by sensory organs called proprioceptors, which can be found in skeletal muscles, tendons, and joints. Along with the vestibular system (the sensory system that provides a sense of balance and spatial orientation), proprioception informs our overall sense of body position, movement effort, and speed, thereby guiding our actions. In other words, proprioception helps us move through the world, interacting with other bodies in ways that allow us to connect and have an impact.

As is true across all our senses, we don't all possess the same degree of proprioceptive awareness, nor are we all able to move in the same way. Movement limitations, variations, and preferences are part of the natural spectrum of human anatomical and physiological diversity. Our proprioceptive capacities can also be affected by injury and misuse. Although the science of measuring proprioception is not well developed, there are a few subjective self-assessments that can help you get a better grasp of your sensory capacities in this domain. If you have trouble with balance or coordination or have a hard time judging the effort required to accomplish a motor task (picking up an object, for example), then you might benefit from activities that help with proprioception. Yoga, dance, sports, martial arts, and countless other movement practices are all excellent for improving our ability to move with more skill and ease.

However, the goal in terms of this book is not better coordination or an expanded movement repertoire. Rather, the intention is to reclaim our ability to *feel* the movements we're doing, not just perform them more deftly or gracefully. The most highly trained ballerina who can execute a dozen flawless pirouettes but who treats her body as an object to be disciplined and controlled is not our role model here. Instead, the key is how we approach the movement practices we engage in. Are we focused exclusively on the goal of a movement, or can we also attend to the process of moving? Do we measure accomplishment solely by how far we stretch or how long we hold a pose, or do we see movement practices as an opportunity to luxuriate in the sensations of speed, strength, effort, and articulation?

When we cultivate the ability to be present in our body while we're moving, we enrich and expand our options. When we're able to *feel our movements* (not just execute them), we open up the possibility of adding depth, nuance, and sensitivity to how we move through the world. These expanded movement possibilities have a direct impact on how perceptively and responsively we navigate the nonverbal dimensions of our everyday interactions with others. Given that so much of our interpersonal communication occurs on this level, being able to sense how our body is moving can make a real difference in shifting power dynamics, establishing rapport, and setting boundaries. Chapter 4 offers additional material on how tuning into our movement can support an activism rooted in our relational engagements and entanglements with other bodies.

EMBODIED PRAXIS
Exploring the Kinesphere

Kinesphere is a movement term coined by choreographer and movement analyst Rudolph Laban. It refers to the roughly spherical space around our body that extends as far as we can reach while remaining stationary. Our kinesphere remains imperceptible until we move within it, filling it with the spatial traces of our movements. Everyone's kinesphere is a little different, depending on the unique reach of our limbs. Taking time to explore our kinesphere can allow us to play with different movement qualities and support the feeling of occupying the space directly around us.

Find a place to stand, sit, or lie comfortably. Exploring your kinesphere while standing up will offer access to the most space and a larger kinesphere, but if standing is not possible or comfortable for you, then sitting or lying will also work just fine. Again, we're aiming for a quality of attentiveness and presence, not quantity of volume. Take a moment to notice your connection to the surface that supports you and the weight of your body in relation to gravity. Ease into that connection, and take a breath or two.

When you're comfortably settled, slowly begin moving your arms, your legs, and your head in a way that plays with the space around you. Notice the reach of each limb and the sensation of reaching. Notice how your relationship with gravity shifts as you move. When you've explored the periphery of your kinesphere, begin playing with the space inside it—in front of your body, behind it, and to each side. What places in your kinesphere feel comfortable and familiar? What places feel strange or uncomfortable? How much of your kinesphere do you typically occupy in your everyday life?

When you've had a chance to explore the volume of your kinesphere, begin experimenting with different ways of moving within it. Play with quick, sharp movements as well as languorous, flowing movements. Alternate light, soft movements with strong, heavy movements. Support these movements with your breath and by anchoring into gravity. Notice the varying sensations these movements elicit. Can you feel your bones articulating at the joints and your muscles sliding over one another? What other feelings arise as you move? Make sure to keep breathing as you move.

As you bring your movement to a close, take a moment to reflect on the difference between moving in this attentive, sensual, present-centered way and how you usually move through the world. Are there ways of moving that you were able to enjoy in this practice but that do not feel safe or acceptable out in the world?

Exteroception: Sensing the World

Exteroception refers to the perception of stimuli arising from outside the body. The term encompasses the classic five senses of sight, hearing, smell, taste, and touch. While we all have varying degrees of acuity across these five sensory domains, each of us tends to have preferred channels for gathering information about our environment. Some of these preferences appear to be innate, while others are learned through experience and socialization. For example, sight and hearing are often highly privileged sensory input channels, while the sense of touch can be overlooked and underdeveloped due to cultural taboos. The following body story offers a glimpse of how smell (another crucial but typically undervalued exteroceptive sense) has featured in the sensual life of a retired biologist named Maya.

BODY STORY
Where the Wild Smells Are

Maya describes herself as a "sucker for a good smell." There is something primal about scent that appeals to her. Consequently, she is often drawn to smells that evoke experiences of the natural world. Maya loves the smell of wood smoke, trees, and freshly cut hay because they remind her of being outdoors in settings where nature and human bodies intersect in pleasurable ways—around a blazing campfire on a cool summer night, wandering along a country road at the edges of a farmer's field, or immersed in the quiet green hush of a city park. Maya has a very well-developed scent memory and can correctly identify smells that she hasn't encountered in decades. She recalls scents in much the same way that one might retain a visual memory. Maya attributes this capacity to her deep links to the natural sensory world.

"It's kind of like with dogs," she says. "Dogs have this amazing ability to smell things that humans can't. With me, I can also smell things that most humans can't, although not nearly as much as dogs. What happens when you can smell really well is that smell becomes more important. It plays a greater role in shaping my experience, including the identification of certain experiences with their corresponding smells, and the recall of those experiences based on smell. For example, my dog died over fifteen years ago. I can still precisely recall the smell of her fur and the smell of the pads of her feet, where there are a lot of specialized scent glands. The smell of her and the feel of her are a lot more important to my memory of her than the image of her."

Because our exteroceptive senses are oriented to the outside world, we use them to scan the environment for possible threats and to locate needed resources. They are the workhorses of our sensory faculties, and a lot of our metabolic energy is directed toward fueling them. Living in hostile or impoverished environments—which are conditions typically found in oppressive social systems—can require a hypervigilant use of these senses, resulting in constriction and exhaustion. Yet, reclaiming our sensual selves as an act of resistance against percepticide involves a rediscovery of all our senses, even those that may feel overused. The embodied praxis exercise below invites us to engage our exteroceptive senses in a way that's undiluted by forced habit and freed of the demands of safety and utility, allowing us to see the world with fresh eyes and listen with open ears. It invites us to taste the world, breathing in its scents and feeling into its textures.

EMBODIED PRAXIS
Sensing the World

Choose a place that's familiar to you—perhaps somewhere in your home or workplace—where you can spend ten minutes exploring your environment undisturbed. Try to find a place where you feel safe and comfortable enough to allow the world to come into you in a new way. Beginning with one sense and then expanding to include the others you have access to, explore this place as if you've never been here before, and you don't have names and purposes for everything you encounter. Instead, allow yourself to soak up the world around you as if it were composed only of colors, shapes, textures, smells, tastes, and sounds. Pick up familiar objects and examine them with the curiosity of a child. What do you notice as you tune in? What happens on the inside of your body when you allow the outside to engage your senses in this way?

Virginia Woolf once famously said, "Thinking is my fighting." While the power of thinking—especially thinking at the margins by the marginalized—continues to be a crucial force for change in an unjust world, this chapter highlights another powerful way to transform oppressive societies: by reclaiming the sensory birthright that has been stolen from us through the commodification and objectification of our bodies. That said, sensory reclaiming is rarely a straightforward process; it can be hampered by internalized ableism and prejudice against sensory differences and complicated by a trauma history that requires a degree of numbing and disconnection from sensation just to cope. Folks with chronic pain or illness may struggle to find places in their bodies that can safely feel pleasure. And of course, we don't all have access to the same set of senses. Despite those challenges, creating a world that allows us to live fully requires some anchoring of that aliveness in our own bodies. In the hidden pockets of our sensory worlds, in a finger or a foot, in a whisper of breath or a rush of color that hits the eye, *feeling* can be our fighting.

4

Rewriting Body Language

This chapter explores the links between embodiment and activism by examining how our body language shapes (and is shaped by) power differences in our social interactions. It offers a conceptual foundation for understanding the role of body language in activism by unpacking how we interpret and respond to the various nonverbal cues of others across a range of interpersonal power dynamics.

Although our body conveys most of the meaning of our communications with one another, we often pay more attention to the words we speak than to the body movement that underscores, elaborates, and (sometimes) contradicts our verbal messages. As psychologist Paul Ekman would argue, most of us don't really know what we're doing with our bodies when we're interacting with others, and we've learned to disregard the internal cues that inform our body movements and facial expressions.[1] Because most nonverbal behavior seems to be enacted with little conscious awareness or choice, our body language can be a prime site for leaking implicit bias and reproducing inequitable power dynamics.

Drawing on research in the field of nonverbal communication, this chapter outlines five elements most relevant to an embodied activism: kinesics (the use of gesture, posture, and facial expression), proxemics (the use of interpersonal space), haptics (the use of touch), oculesics (the use of eye contact), and object communication (how we use objects such as clothing and furniture to convey socially significant messages). These components are then linked to key areas where power differences often show up, including through embodied microaggressions. Last, we explore how our nonverbal communication can be interrogated, liberated, and rewritten so that our interactions with one another can become more consciously respectful, authentic, powerful, compassionate, and fair.

Communication between human beings is a complex, dynamic, contested, contingent, and contextually dependent system. Researchers have defined communication as a "dynamic and ongoing process whereby people create shared meaning through the sending and receiving of messages via commonly understood codes".[2] It involves all modes of sending and receiving messages and draws on innate reflexive characteristics, such as a newborn baby's instinct to turn toward a touch on its cheek, as well as learned behaviors, such as the complex but meaningful hand gestures in traditional Balinese dance forms.

Nonverbal communication can be broadly defined as all the messages that people exchange during their interactions with one another, conveyed in means other than words. Although we typically don't pay much attention to these messages, they are both potent and plentiful. We have the capacity to produce nearly three-quarters of a million distinct physical signs, including different bodily postures, hand gestures, and facial expressions. When interpersonal communication is conceived of as a matrix containing different types of behavior, nonverbal communication can then be defined as the process in which nonverbal behaviors are used to exchange and interpret messages within a given situation. At times these nonverbal cues are used to modify or underscore a verbal message, while on other occasions they replace verbal communication entirely.

Although we rarely focus on these nonverbal dimensions of communication when we review or analyze our interpersonal communications—such as when we're rehashing an argument we had with a friend—their significance to the overall message is considerable. Conservative estimates suggest that about 65 percent of a message's meaning is communicated through these nonverbal clues, while others assert that up to 90 percent of the emotional meaning of a message is transmitted nonverbally. The importance of nonverbal communication is further demonstrated by the finding that when verbal and nonverbal cues are used together, nonverbal cues have over four times the impact of verbal cues.[3] Moreover, the embodied dimension of interpersonal communication is consistently experienced as more "truthful" than the actual words spoken.[4] When faced with a contradiction between the verbal content of a message and its nonverbal counterpart, it's the body's message that we believe.

Given the significance of the nonverbal element of interpersonal communication, it makes sense to attend to it as a crucial component of power relations between people. Experts argue that nonverbal communication affects our relationships and interpersonal environments in intricate ways, providing insight into emotional states and influencing perceptions of competence, sincerity, authority, and vulnerability. Despite its importance in human interaction, many of us don't really know what we're doing with our bodies when we're engaging with others, and no one tells us. We've learned to disregard the constant stream of body movements and facial expressions we make, and we seem to have little conscious awareness of or choice about what our body is saying to others.

It could be argued that this lack of awareness is indicative of a level of somatic illiteracy common to modern Western society, in which the contribution the body makes to our overall life experience is largely unacknowledged. The study of nonverbal communication attempts to address this deficiency by offering insight into those aspects of interpersonal communication for which the body is the primary medium. Although the field has classified these elements into several categories, only the five areas most applicable to embodied activism will be explored here.

Posture, Gesture, and Facial Expression

Kinesics is the study of nonverbal communication related to movement—all kinds of movement, large or small, from any part of the body. From finger pointing to foot tapping, from chronic slouching to facial microexpressions lasting a fraction of a second, we learn to track the kinesic behavior of others as diligently as we listen to their words, even if we may not be conscious of doing so. The meanings communicated through these body movements vary widely; cultural and gender differences in gestures are common, and there is no international language of gestures. Instead, cultures have developed systems of unique gestures, so that it is often not possible to understand the gestures from another culture without some prior exposure or orientation.

In fact, gestures that are acceptable in one culture may be offensive in another culture. For example, in Western societies, putting one's feet up on a sofa or footstool in the presence of others usually indicates a positive level of trust and camaraderie. In many Arabic countries, however, this gesture may be understood as insulting because it's offensive to show others the soles of your feet. Similarly, a friendly pat on the head would likely be considered impolite to a Tibetan Buddhist monk. Even between members of the same culture or identity group, kinesic behavior can be misinterpreted. Unfortunately, this openness to interpretation can also serve as a camouflage for disrespect, such as when someone falsely insists their insolent behavior has been misread.

As a result, the embodied relationships upon which an everyday activism depends are often complicated by the underlying dynamics being unconsciously conveyed and reinforced by our posture, gestures, and facial expressions. If we want these relationships to serve as the foundation of sustainable social transformation, then attending to this dimension of interpersonal communication is crucial. The first step of such attending is simply to notice how much we move our bodies when we're engaging with others and to realize how much we track the movements of others to help us know how the interaction is going.

EMBODIED PRAXIS
Tuning into the Kinesic Flow

The next time you're interacting with someone, take a moment to tune into the silent dance of movements that accompany your conversation. William Condon calls this rhythmic flow of nonverbal communication *interactional synchrony*—when everyone's body is accompanying the flow of their own words but also somehow interacting with the movements of others. No need to analyze or interpret the meaning of particular gestures, postures, or facial expressions; just notice the dance. What kinds of movements catch your attention, and how does it feel in your body to attend to them? Then notice if there are places where the dance falters, when someone fails to respond to a cue or interrupts the rhythm in some way. Again, no judgment. At this point, you're just practicing tuning into how our bodies participate in our relationships through movement, so that when you want to interrogate, shift, or disrupt these patterns, you'll be more comfortable navigating the kinesic flow.

If you have the opportunity, watch a video of yourself interacting with others, but with the sound turned off. What do you notice about the nonverbal dance of postures, gestures, and facial expressions when it's foregrounded in this way?

The Eyes Have It

Oculesics refers to the study of the use of eye movement to communicate with others. This includes eye contact (or the avoidance of eye contact), but it also includes other eye movements, such as looking at parts of the other person or at other features of the environment. Research suggests that the eyes have directive features; for example, when a speaker suddenly looks to the side of the room, their audience will typically look there as well. Eye movement and eye contact are also used to discourage or encourage affiliation or attention. Gazing steadily into the eyes of another person can be remarkably intimate—so much so that some research suggests the act itself can *create* bonds, not just reflect them.[5]

However, like other forms of nonverbal communication, the way in which the eyes are used to communicate can vary widely across cultures.[6] For example, in some cultures people lower their gaze to convey respect, but in other cultures this behavior may be understood as evasive or insulting. Conversely, some cultures may see direct eye contact as offensive, whereas in others it indicates respectful attention.

EMBODIED PRAXIS
Noticing Gaze

Choose a situation in which you can comfortably observe the eye movement and eye contact behavior of people in a small-group setting—perhaps a work meeting or a family gathering where you can step back from the flow of interaction and just notice who looks where and for how long. Are there group members who get a lot of eye contact from the rest of the group? Are there members who aren't being looked at, or who aren't looking at others? Does the eye movement behavior you're witnessing correspond in some way to your sense of the group dynamics—for example, who the leader is, where the bonds of affiliation lie, or who the outcasts or marginal members are?

Then gradually begin to notice your own eye movement behavior in this setting. Who do you look at? Who do you avoid looking at or forget to look at? Are you making direct eye contact with anyone? Is that comfortable or uncomfortable for you? Do your eye movements align with your feelings of participation and belonging in the group? And last, do these patterns of eye gazing feel familiar or seem typical to you? As best you can, approach this exercise in the spirit of curiosity and nonjudgment, for both yourself and others. Just notice what's there.

Getting in Touch

Touch is a primal form of communication that is necessary to our neurological and social development.[7] Without nurturing touch, we struggle to thrive, and yet the wrong kind of touch can cause profound harm. Regardless of our personal touch histories, how we navigate touching others in our social interactions can be complex and loaded. Although touching is most frequent during greetings and departures—handshakes, kissing, fist-bumping, and hugging—it can occur throughout our interactions with others.

Touching is often (but not always) an indicator of the degree of informality or intimacy in a relationship, and the use of touch to reflect and enact various degrees of intimacy may change from one individual to the next, as well as across cultures. For example, researchers who recorded touching behaviors involved in interpersonal communication across several different cultures found that in England, France, and the Netherlands, touching was relatively rare compared to Italy and Greece. Social touch customs vary widely; for example, Latinos often greet each other with a hug and a kiss on one cheek, many Europeans kiss on both cheeks, and people from Arabic countries often do three kisses. The use of touch in social interactions also varies according to gender and age (for example, women and children typically get touched more than adult men).[8]

Regardless of how we learned to use touch to communicate, this form of nonverbal communication typically carries the strongest taboos and social sanctions. As a result, we often receive a lot of explicit instruction from our families, teachers, friends, and work settings about how to handle touch in interpersonal contexts. Sometimes these directives conflict with our own innate preferences, and not infrequently they contradict each other. So, navigating touch in interpersonal relationships can be fraught at any stage of socioemotional development and across a wide range of social contexts.

BODY STORY
Navigating Touch Differences at Work

I once had a dear colleague who was a devout Muslim. We worked in a large Western university where we interacted with dozens of different people, often meeting several new people over the course of a typical workday. One day I was hanging out in his office chatting about various shared topics of interest and generally catching up when I noticed that his fingers were covered with small adhesive bandages. Concerned that he had hurt himself, I asked if his hands were okay. He looked uncomfortable at first and then confessed to me that he had decided to put bandages on his hands as way to avoid shaking hands with people. As a practicing Muslim, he was raised to refrain from touching women outside his own family yet was regularly confronted with female colleagues who offered a handshake as a form of greeting. He had grown tired of explaining his own cultural practices around touch to every new person he met, so he came upon this strategy of bandaging his hands so he could avoid a handshake by pointing at the bandages as an excuse not to touch.

I thought about this for a little while and realized that my own neurodiversity-based touch avoidance meant that I rarely offered a handshake to anyone, neatly avoiding placing my friend in the social dilemma of having to refuse my touch. It wasn't until I noticed the bandages that the topic came up between us. A little while later, I realized that despite my being out as genderqueer, my colleague probably still read me as female, which could explain why he had never offered to shake my hand, as I had seen him do with male colleagues.

EMBODIED REFLECTION AND INTEGRATION
Getting in Touch

What are some of your own personal touch preferences? Do you feel comfortable expressing and enacting them in various social settings, or is there some tension or discomfort around touch? How were you taught to handle touch growing up? Were social norms of touch taught to you through explicit instruction, or did you simply follow the touch customs of the culture in which you were raised? Are there ways of navigating touch that you'd like to shift?

Navigating Interpersonal Space

Proxemics is the study of our perception and use of interpersonal space. The term was coined by anthropologist Edward T. Hall to describe the measurable distances between people as they interacted. He observed that individuals unconsciously establish a comfortable distance for different types of personal interaction, and they nonverbally define this as their personal space: "intimate distance" for embracing, touching, or whispering; "personal distance" for interactions among close friends; "social distance" for interactions among acquaintances; and "public distance" used for public speaking.[9]

Modifying the distance between two people can suggest a desire for intimacy, assert a lack of interest, or signal domination, and violation of this personal space can have adverse effects on feelings of trust and rapport. Like the other types of nonverbal communication, the use of space varies across culture, gender, age, and other social factors. There is no one correct distance between people. Ideally, the management of space between people involves a mutual navigation and negotiation of how to share the space that respects differing preferences. Proxemics is also concerned with physical territory, or the way we arrange objects in space to communicate relationships, such as placing a throne on a dais raised above the rest of the court or having students' desks face the front of a classroom.

> ## EMBODIED PRAXIS
> ### Body Boundaries
>
> The next time you find yourself standing talking with someone, notice how much space exists between your bodies. Is this a comfortable amount of space between you? How do you know this—which bodily indicators signal comfort or discomfort? Which factors contribute to your feelings of comfort or discomfort? If the space between you is uncomfortable for you, how could you make it more comfortable?
>
> The next time you're in a group setting, notice how the space is configured. Are people sitting, or are they standing in clusters? How has the furniture been arranged? What do those arrangements tell you about the relationships between the people in the room?
>
> Paying attention to the somatic dimensions of physical boundaries can often give us information about psychological and emotional boundaries as well. We can feel intruded upon, abandoned, or supported by others without our physical space being involved, but these other forms of boundary issues can evoke very similar bodily responses. Similarly, setting physical space boundaries can help us build the relational "muscles" to set other kinds of boundaries as well.

Nonverbal Communication as Social Control

Given the power of nonverbal communication to influence perception and transform the meaning of our verbal exchanges, it's perhaps not surprising that social power dynamics are very commonly transmitted through this medium.[10] In fact, feminist communication experts Nancy Henley and Jo Freeman argue that the most common means of social control is not institutional structure; it's the nonverbal component of social interaction.[11] Through a form of silent policing, members of socially stigmatized groups are constantly reminded of our inferior social status through the nonverbal messages we receive from others. We are also required to affirm that status in our response to those messages (for example, smiling or looking away), as well as in the messages we ourselves trans-mit (for example, using muted gestures or taking up little space).

These patterns are taught both explicitly through instruction and implicitly through modeling within and across social groups. Sometimes, this schooling in knowing your place is transmitted through forms of social punishment—ostracism, ridicule, and bullying—enacted by members of a dominant social group. Other times, learning how to enact the body language of submission occurs within members of the same social group as a protective strategy. For example, Black parents in the United States and Europe routinely teach their children how to survive encounters with the authorities. "The talk" provides a detailed set of instructions for how to perform the kinds of nonverbal behavior intended to deescalate police reactivity when being stopped and questioned by an officer: not making any sudden movements, not staring, keeping your hands where they can be seen, and nodding in agreement even if you disagree. Many women learn a similar set of nonverbal deescalation techniques for dealing with harassment by men that includes smiling and lowering their gaze as a nonverbal appeasement strategy.

Of course, it's crucial to take into account the significant cultural variations of these nonverbal signals. There is widespread acknowledgement in the field of nonverbal communication that our body language is as culturally varied as our spoken language. Even within cultures, we vary in our use of nonverbal strate-gies to convey power. Regardless of these variations, it's possible to identify a few underlying dynamics that shape how many of us navigate power through our embodied interactions with one another. Examining these embodied practices of oppression reveals two key patterns: the presence of asymmetrical interactions and the use of dominant/submissive kinesic behavior.

Asymmetrical Interaction

A key feature of the nonverbal-communication patterns between individuals with differing social status or authority is unequal access to certain behav-iors related to informality and intimacy. In these asymmetrical interactions, the person with more power has the "right" to exercise certain familiarities that the subordinated person is not permitted to initiate or reciprocate. For example, in conversation with an employee, a supervisor may lean back in their chair in a relatively casual and relaxed posture, while their employee is expected to maintain a more formal stance and demeanor. That same supervisor may touch their employee casually on the arm while making a conversational point, but the employee does not have the same license to initiate touch with their supervisor.

The right to interpersonal space provides another example of asymmetrical nonverbal interaction. Early studies in nonverbal communication showed that dominant animals and high-status human beings are afforded greater personal space, and those with lower status are expected to yield space to those with higher status. For example, research suggests that men are more likely to invade women's personal space than vice versa.[12]

Likewise, eye contact is also employed dissimilarly along lines of power difference in social interactions. Members of socially subordinated groups tend to look more at those they regard as sources of social approval, yet they may lower or avert their gaze when a high-status individual looks back at them. In contrast, staring is widely believed to be the prerogative of those in dominant social roles.[13]

Signaling Dominance and Submission

Research in nonverbal communication also suggests that a particular set of gestures and postures are associated with social power and dominance, such as pointing, staring, and holding the head erect, while those in subordinated positions tend to employ movements more suggestive of submission, such as nodding, lowering eyes, and bowing or tilting the head. Smiling has also been offered as an important example of submissive kinesic behavior. Feminist activist Shulamith Firestone contends that women smile at men not because they are happy, but as a conciliatory gesture.[14] (Firestone also proposed a "smile boycott" as a direct action against gender oppression.) Later research has reinforced the assertion that subordinated individuals smile more in social situations, regardless of their emotional state.

Overall, the research on nonverbal communication suggests that in situations in which one group is seen as inferior to another, members of the ostensibly inferior group will typically be more nonverbally submissive, more sensitive (attuned to and accurate in decoding another's nonverbal expressions), and more accommodating (adapting to another's nonverbal behaviors). The repetitive and insidious nature of these everyday exercises in dominance and submission may cause them to slip below our level of awareness, such that we effectively internalize social conventions and power relations to the point where they may become normalized and almost unremarkable.[15] And, of course, when we're not aware of how our bodies are participating in the systems of oppression we're trapped in, it's not possible to harness the potency of our bodily gestures to resist and transform those systems.

EMBODIED REFLECTION AND INTEGRATION
Noticing Social Power in Body Language

Are there nonverbal behaviors that you do not feel entitled or allowed to enact based on your membership in a subordinated social group? Conversely, are there nonverbal behaviors you feel perfectly comfortable engaging in, even though you suspect others might not feel as comfortable? Might your comfort be related to social privilege? Does your access to certain kinds of body language change depending on the context you're in?

Understanding the significance of our nonverbal communication in the context of interpersonal power dynamics provides an important basis for appreciating the role of the body in reproducing social patterns of inequity. This kind of understanding suggests pathways and practices that support our bodies in becoming a necessary foundation for our activism. However, just because certain movements, gestures, or postures are associated with social power, it is important for those of us who experience oppression not to feel pressure to automatically adopt those nonverbal patterns as a route to empowerment. It would be a mistake to assume that such "power moves" are automatically better and that it is the oppressed who should change. In other words, rewriting our body language as a strategy of liberation and social transformation requires that we unpack and interrogate this wordless dance of power that runs like a perpetual background track through our lives. Then we can make our own choices.

So, what might this all look like as a form of everyday embodied activism? The following interview with my colleague Christine Caldwell offers some strategies for liberating our body movement in ways that can help shift old patterns of dominance/submission and allow new movement impulses to be generated and expressed.

Liberating our Movement: An Interview with Christine Caldwell[16]

Rae: Christine, what would you like to share with readers who are interested in engaging their own movement to explore the possibilities of being less bound by the forces of oppression that have shaped their bodies? What does liberating your movement mean to you?

Christine: I would say that movement exists along a continuum, from very small cellular movement all the way to whole-body movement and then social interactional movement. But there is a second continuum of movement that can be mapped onto the first one. Scholars in the biology of movement talk about a mobility gradient that goes from what they call constrained movement to free movement. Constrained movement is much like cellular movement, such as automatic muscle reflexes that we're not necessarily monitoring and movements that we're not necessarily in control of, even if we can monitor them. This continuum then extends all the way to very free and unconstrained kinds of movement. For me, the short answer to what movement liberation means is that there are these two continuums, from very tiny to really large, and also from constrained to less constrained, that we should be free to move along as circumstances shift. In other words, I see liberated movement as the ability to go across these continuums adaptively and in a way that promotes one's own bodily integrity and bodily authority.

Rae: In addition to bodily integrity and bodily authority, would you add the criterion of interactional effectiveness?

Christine: That's a great question. This is something that I'm working out, particularly how we understand movement as language and movement as communication. So that is a really important lens to put on what we're talking about. Let's start with the idea of expression. For example, when you hit your thumb with a hammer and you go "Ow!," that's literally expressing. The movement is pressing out of you, and it's not taking into consideration getting received or understood by someone out there. It's just coming out. So that particular kind of movement is a little bit raw, and it's very critical for our well-being to understand how that works. But when we move toward wanting our expressiveness to be understood, we have a tendency—either subliminally or consciously—to adapt our movement so it can be understood. We shape it into coherent messages. What's interesting is how the moving body acts as a communicative device. And if I think of liberation, I don't think it completely maps onto this idea of being understood by someone else, of interactional effectiveness.

There's a political issue that is being debated a lot in communications theory that has to do with who has the responsibility for coherency. In other words, do I have to bear all the burden of moving until you get me? Or is there some responsibility on your part to make an effort to translate my movement into something that helps you feel connected to me? So that's where it starts to be about movement being effective. And the word *effective* starts getting interesting.

Rae: I guess what I was thinking about with interactional effectiveness has more to do with the nonverbal-communication research on how being a member of a socially subordinated group tends to result in being less freely expressive yet more alert to other people's expressiveness. Being better at reading body language, but less able to be completely unconstrained in our own body language. Does liberating our movement have something to do with the freedom to communicate in body language as fully, honestly, and authentically as others do, or as we might want? So when you said the goal of liberating movement is agency and bodily authority, I wondered about the interactional, social, and cultural aspects of that. From your perspective, is liberated movement also movement that has some sense of social power?

Christine: Yes. As we know from the research, our own and that of others, in subordinated groups there's this whole idea of code-switching. So, you have to know multiple body languages and you have to be bilingual or trilingual on a somatic level in order to navigate an oppressive environment. And so we're not at what we might call "liberation" if that's still happening. When you are in a subordinated group, you are the one that is burdened with being understood. You have to translate your movement into something that is deemed acceptable by the person in power. So you alter your movement behavior in order to stay safe, in order to be understood, in order to connect, et cetera. Whereas the person with more power doesn't need to do that to anywhere near the same extent.

Rae: They don't need to translate or adapt.

Christine: Exactly. It's very parallel to the verbal level. People in power don't have to code-switch.

Rae: Right. Also parallel to the verbal level, of course, is the fact that one of the things that we know about colonized social groups is that they lose their language. Native language is deliberately exterminated.

Christine: Yes, exactly.

Rae: I wonder if you have thoughts about members of socially subordinated groups having their body language exterminated. Perhaps it's not even a matter of code-switching. There is no authentic movement repertoire to return to, as a result of being socialized into a system where the original cultural body language was not permitted.

Christine: It gets lost. Take, for instance, the Native American languages that got squashed at the Indian residential schools. I think this is exactly what happens. So that one's movement culture is either appropriated and/or exterminated.

Rae: And perhaps one's "authentic" movement preferences might have been so thoroughly colonized that someone in the process of wanting to liberate their movement might even not know where to begin.

Christine: Native American author Sherman Alexie talks about his mother being one of the last speakers of the West Coast Salish language. He said that at the time of her death, his mother told him that English was his future. I think it's important to acknowledge what's lost. I'm thinking about this a lot lately in terms of storytelling and how the body is a storyteller. I think about my own father's stories and how they are getting altered and lost over time. There's this inevitable loss that I think is part of the normal death of a generation. And it allows for new body stories to emerge, new ways of moving to be developed and owned. But what you are bringing up is different, because we are not talking about the natural death process. We are talking about extermination. Physical bodies are exterminated, and physical cultures are exterminated.

Something I've been really interested in lately is this huge movement on TikTok to post one's own dances. You develop some dance moves in your bedroom, and you post them on TikTok. One of the emerging issues is that dance moves created by African American teenagers are being appropriated by White girls who then monetize them through endorsements. As a result, there's now this countermove to credit where you learned the dance moves from, to support these young Black women who are creating movement that is celebratory and danced by hundreds of thousands of people across the world. This is a kind of liberation movement that is also trying to deal with appropriation. The idea is that these body stories keep evolving. Yes, a lot has been destroyed and will never come back. But there is such a strong body liberation movement that is reasserting itself in youth culture and is struggling with social media extermination.

Rae: This reminds me of the sociologist Marcel Mauss talking about "techniques of the body." When cultures are destroyed, their techniques of the body also die—that capacity to weave or carve or sing in a particular way. One of the consequences of the forces of colonization. But what I also hear you saying is that liberating movement is not necessarily about a return to some previous cultural ideal.

Christine: Exactly. Although preserving and recreating historical forms is of course a legitimate activity, I don't think it should be the sole focus or the sole purpose. We have to also include these more recent methodologies for liberation, a lot of which are now live on TikTok and Instagram.

Rae: The power that movement has to create new culture. And how that needs to be seen as equally as important as someone's capacity to reclaim lost or repressed cultures of movement.

Christine: Yes, exactly. So part of liberating one's movement is the freedom to remain creative in one's life and to evolve new movement, and not get criticized for failing to be traditional or "authentic."

Rae: One of the things that I understood from your description of the continuum between constraint and less constraint, or between micro and macro movement, is that the key here is to have a choice about where and how you move.

Christine: Yes.

Rae: And there might be times where quite constrained movement is an effective choice.

Christine: This is something I was hoping we could talk about, because I really want to make sure we don't fall into what I think is probably a White-centric idea that we only want to work toward this kind of unconstrained movement, an ideal to move any way I want and find movement that is very cool and improvisational. There's a place for improvisational movement. But I also want to assert that part of our liberation is to support and work within the framework of constrained movement, because constraining movement is actually really important. It's important for safety and because constrained movement underlies and supports improvisational movement. You can't be spontaneous effectively if you don't have constrained movement supporting it. A lot of folks that are studying movement talk about how reflexes underlie any kind of effective movement, for instance.

Rae: I'm thinking of an analogy to music, where the best jazz improvisers know their scales and chord progressions. They know their musical structures. Practicing constraint and control with their vibrato or their phrasing is what allows them the freedom to improvise well. Jazz improvisation is not just this free-for-all loosey-goosey thing. And so, I guess it would be a mistake to think of liberated body movement as only being completely uncontrolled and uncontained.

Christine: Yes, exactly. Because the more you do that kind of far-out improvisational expressivity, the less you are able to actually connect with others. Connecting with others involves a kind of ongoing body shaping. In terms of bodily well-being and fitness, the ability to move in rote ways has some real advantages. It's also connected to how Mihaly Csikszentmihalyi talks about the flow state, where discipline and limits are an integral part of how flow states are generated. This is really interesting when we get into this idea. I was so enculturated as a child of the 1960s to think of less constrained and more improvisational movement as better.

Rae: And more liberated.

Christine: This is the rabbit hole we do not want to fall into.

Rae: Because it isn't more liberated if it's really your only peer-endorsed choice.

Christine: Right. It's not sustainable from either an interior perspective or a social perspective.

Rae: To bring the jazz music metaphor up again, the best improvisers also know how to listen.

Christine: Because they're listening—the sax is listening to the vibes, which is listening to the bass—there's an evolving structure that is emergent.

Rae: It raises the question of scale. And choices about scale and repetition and how repetition can be useful in creating structure.

Christine: Yes, yes, exactly. It's fascinating and not surprising that you said that, because I'm learning about movement and scale and how there are some fundamental scaling laws that seem to repeat across physics, chemistry, biology, sociology, and social systems. I get really attracted to ways of thinking that seem like they radiate out into other disciplines. Because for me, I think movement is actually one of the most cross-disciplinary things we can ever talk about or play with. Everything moves.

Rae: So, we've touched on some of the challenges of movement liberation as a form of activism; one of them concerns automatically assuming that liberating movement means larger scale and less constrained movement rather than the choice to move across the continuum between micro and macro and between degrees of containment. Are there other challenges when you've worked with others in the process of liberating their movement to help them access more choice as a result of their own history of oppression?

Christine: I'll invoke the philosopher Elizabeth Benhke and her concept of sedimentation. She talks about past trauma and social forces being sedimented in the body, causing the body to be more colonized. She didn't use the word *colonization,* but I would. There's a kind of natural sedimentation that I think is unavoidable in terms of all of us being our ancestors' offspring. There's no getting around that, and we might as well relax about it. But in oppressive systems, there's a kind of sedimentation that is systemic and traumatic. What I see clinically is that it goes underground. There's this sense of the person not even realizing the sedimentation or the colonization of their body—how it's tightening certain muscles, fixing facial expressions, or compressing the body. And it's altering time, space, and force in the body so that it has a cost that is constantly being paid because of trauma and oppression.

What I see clinically is that people frequently experience this sedimentation as their identity. We are looking at how the body generates identity. For example, when I wake up in the morning, I have that familiar kind of tension in my shoulders. That's how I know I'm Christine—that and about five other things that I track when I'm waking up. There's this body identity that occurs and of course is normal and ongoing and hopefully is fluid and adaptable. I can wake up one way one morning and another way another morning, but that doesn't start to happen in a colonized body. The body's always waking up the same way, and it begins to identify with that. It's like internalized oppression. And so, the movement is expressive of internalized oppression. What can be interesting is how to help someone really feel how sedimented that movement is and to begin to try to question whether that's an identity that feels like the costs and benefits of it are working out the way you want.

It's not that you want to get rid of any kind of ongoing bodily identity; it's that you want to make sure it benefits you. Clinically, my work in the Moving Cycle is first to really feel it the way it is; to really enter into, "Oh, this; I feel compelled to keep doing this." And instead of trying to not do it, I actually keep doing it deliberately and consciously. Such as, for example, letting the chest go down, a tendency to collapse in my chest. So instead of making that wrong and calling it colonization, I allow that to occur with more consciousness. And when I allow it to occur with this really high-quality attention, then that's the first step to liberation—this high-quality attention. All the while not trying to change it yet. Not trying to make it different, but to really experience the nuance of that sedimentation. The second phase would be that when you participate with it instead of trying to get rid of it, different associations come up. So, you are allowing images, sounds, words, memories, feelings, and other movement impulses to emerge and to begin to play with that sedimentation on their own. Instead of explanation, we look at association. We braid in the body's natural abilities to work with sedimentation so that it kind of fluffs up, you know. It becomes less dense, it becomes more porous, and then it becomes more move-able in novel directions. So now these associations are able to direct my move-ment into a direction that feels right rather than a sedimenting one. I'm curious what you think about that.

Rae: What I'm hearing in this process of witnessing the sedimentation of my own body is that it allows some of the layers of sedimentation to peel back or to lift a little bit so that it's more spacious. I can actually see the layers rather than just experience the net effect of decades and generations of sedimentation. I now have the possibility of just being with it in an impartial, accepting, notic-ing way, with this high-quality attention. Now I can go, "Oh, this layer, that's where that came from." Or, "That's the subtlety, or the shape, or the tone, or the history, of this layer." It seems to me that it's not quite unpacking but instead opening up and lifting the layers of sedimentation to create some more breath-ing room.

Christine: In terms of liberation, I'm wanting to see if there's any kind of subtle "trying" to make it different that could get in the way of really being with it the way it is. This stage needs to be supported before true liberation can occur.

Lately I've been questioning the word *witness*. The traditional definition of "witness" is a kind of other-observing entity. And I'm not sure that that's what happens first. I think it does come in, but I think first there's just raw data that gets accessed by being with it experientially and wholeheartedly. We don't have language for this being with it, being within the experience without trying to also hover over it or be outside it.

Rae: We're feeling into it. We're more than observing. I might offer the term "accompanying" to suggest it's not this impartial observation.

Christine: I think one of the things that interfere with liberation is a rush to meaning-making. The liberating experience is not only being able to talk about one's experience to others. It begins in this kind of raw data gathering where you're just opening out to more and more and more of the details of the experience. You're not foreclosing on it by packaging it. I talk about that as postponing meaning-making.

Rae: Because you're not trying to fix it.

Christine: Yes, exactly. There's a time for fixing. It's not that we don't want to, but it's that the liberation really becomes full-bodied when we can really rest into this "being with it the way it is" space first. Otherwise, liberation is just some version of the next thing that you're supposed to sediment in, whether it's a kind of liberal, progressive attitude or a certain kind of vocabulary that will help you identify as a liberated person or a feminist or whatever is progressive. So that blurring of the old identity actually involves a kind of letting go of any identity for a little bit of time, which occurs when we occupy the experience we are having with discipline but without control, and we let a new identity emerge on its own from the body.

Rae: Otherwise, we're looking at what body sociologist Chris Shilling would call the "body as a project" of self-improvement.

Christine: Yes, perfect. And self-improvement from that perspective isn't liberation.

Rae: A top-down "liberation" of movement.

Christine: Equally controlling and colonizing in its own way.

Rae: Trying to undo something currently existing in order to "improve" it and overlay a different set of cultural norms. And in some cases, we might be forcing a countercultural norm of what so-called enlightened, woke people "should" look like or be like.

Christine: It comes down to who gets to define what's liberated. If the therapist or the activist, or whoever, gets to define what's liberated for you, then we're back at oppression.

Rae: We're just substituting impositions. I'm hearing that you really trust the body's capacity to generate new possibilities and new impulses, that you trust the authenticity of those impulses in the same way you are rightly suspicious of imposed countercultural norms.

Christine: I'm deeply trustful of what the body itself comes up with. However, I don't want to minimize the fact that it can involve time and energy and some aspects of struggle in it. There've been times where I've been in some kind of movement experience and I'll say, "I don't know, this might be just another version of some kind of sedimentation," so authenticity is not necessarily easy to find. And that's why I think that my work has always been on the edges. It demands an uncommon level of commitment and effort. There's a simplicity *and* a complexity to it, and we have to sign up for the complexity as well as the simplicity of this kind of movement liberation. It ain't necessarily easy.

Rae: And not reassuring.

Christine: Yes, exactly. Not comforting.

Rae: Right. You can't say, "If you just do this, you will feel better. You will be freer, and your body will love you for it, and you'll love your body for it. Just overthrow the shackles of oppression and come right this way." So, you don't offer any of that reassurance, and it's possible that our first impulses or hints or nuances or preliminary understandings turn out to be ones that we don't wind up wanting to live with. In fact, we're signing up for a process.

Christine: Nicely put. Signing up for a life. A particular kind of life.

Rae: Where the answers aren't easy or simple, and where you have to do the work of generating them yourself to some extent.

Christine: We commonly think of self-reflection as a cognitive phenomenon, and sure, there are cognitive processes that can go on. But what I get really interested in is self-reflection that does not yet include higher-order cognitive processing. The somatic aspect of my experience has been bullied for millennia by cognitive self-reflection, so I think we need to dedicate a bunch of time and energy to somatic self-reflection. An important aspect of movement liberation is also a liberation from thinking about the movement. In this sense, the body itself deserves reparations, or "repair-ative" movement time.

Rae: I hear you describing a kind of "being with" and "being in" our movement, without any assurance or predetermined goals or objectives. You're not trying to find a solution or necessarily make meaning, but you're learning how to process bodily experience by being in it and considering it, allowing surprises and novelty and uncertainty, and being willing to live with that.

Christine: Yes. We also want to be careful as body-oriented folks not to have a kind of hubris where we assert that the body never lies. We can't put our body on a pedestal in terms of "our body knows all the answers" or "it's always telling the truth." My experience, both in my own movement and in clinical work, is that sometimes people grab onto body states as true.

Rae: I like what you're saying. Perhaps the only way to avoid nailing things down prematurely when we're in a process of liberating our movement is to go in with the clarity that we're not trying to fix anything.

Christine: You're not trying to fix anything, and you're not trying to box it up. Boxing it up at this point is actually antithetical to liberation.

Rae: What else would you want to add to what we've talked about in terms of what you hope a reader might find on these pages?

Christine: We started with the idea of these two continuums: from constrained to unconstrained movement, and then movement at various levels of scale. My ongoing hypothesis is that we want to be able to see some kinds of regularities in the experience and the expression of people who feel like they're on the path of liberation. And what I suspect could happen in these folks is there'll be a kind of a bell curve. On any continuum, we have a tendency to hang out in the middle of the mobility gradient, the middle of the scale, so we may only use highly constrained and highly unconstrained movement on rare occasions. That's fine. That's very organic. What do you think of that? Because certainly on some level we should probably be suspicious of bell curves.

Rae: It seems to me that the process of liberating one's movement maybe also requires the accompanying commitments not just to avoid prematurely imposing meaning and to avoid substituting one form of sedimentation with another, but also to cultivate a capacity to recognize internally when something feels right, authentic, and resonant. I would argue that resonance is maybe also something that doesn't just feel contained within the body but extends outside of the body. You and I have talked before about energy streams and flow. How do we move in a way that feels right and true to us, given the embeddedness of our body in social-cultural and political contexts? Having the time to do some somatic reflection on our own legacy, our own history, our own sedimentation is one thing. But in the interactive everyday moments in our multiple and complex worlds, we're not going to be able to do that. What I think we will need to cultivate and then learn to trust is the feeling of when something is aligned and resonant with who we are. To have a feeling in our body that we learn to listen and feel into so that when we're moving in a liberated way, there's an accompanying sensation of pleasure and rightness. Without that, I don't know how movement liberation can walk its way out of the studio or the ashram and actually make it into the real world.

Christine: Just like in meditation, you have to get up off the cushion and live your life, and it's the same thing. You have to move in society and the outside world. You have to go to the grocery store. This work needs to apply to those things. It needs to be embedded.

Rae: And so, is that true for you? Do you have a sensory touchstone that lets you know what the liberated movement option would be in a particular setting? How do you know?

Christine: There are times where I don't know, and it's important to normalize not knowing and to stay with that and not make it wrong. It is such a profound question. But I feel that in those kinds of moments, those kinds of really deep self-recognition moments, that there's a feeling that I'm both completely there and completely not there. And I get this also as a therapist in sessions. I'll feel this ongoing exchange with the client where I feel like I'm profoundly present, but also not there as well. I'm not sure how much more I can articulate that, but it's feeling that kind of exquisite tension of being both really there, and the "me" is not there. I don't know that it is sensory, or not sensory.

Rae: It sounds to me a little bit like flow.

Christine: I think so too. Csikszentmihalyi had this whole list of opposites that he said the flow state invoked, and although he didn't say "there and not there," I think it needs to be added.

Rae: Both fully present and not present in the embodied ego state that we're used to.

Christine: That's a good way to put it. The normal ego state is relaxed. There's a "me"-ness that is unrecognizable because of how I perform myself so often, but it's also powerfully recognized, like, "yeah." You're both moving and being moved at the same time. That powerful state of me and not-me. It brings up learning how to canoe in white water. What is really disastrous in class III rapids is when you try to overcontrol it: "I want the canoe to be exactly here now, and I'm gonna work really hard." That doesn't work. You just fall in. But it also doesn't work to just take your paddle out of the water and say, "I'm just going to let the river do it," because then we also fall in. There's this working *with* the river. You're putting energy into working with the river. The best canoeists I've ever seen are just brilliant at meeting the way the water is tumbling and working with what's coming up. It's just beautiful.

Rae: That might be as good a phenomenological description of liberated movement as we're going to get to. There are powerful forces and subtle undercurrents that will turn you over. Getting good at liberating your movement means working with those forces so you can direct yourself.

Christine: Moving with.

Rae: But not surrendering to.

Christine: Exactly.

EMBODIED REFLECTION AND INTEGRATION
Liberating Our Movement

What are some of the current constraints on your body movement? How did they originate? Do you experience them in all settings, or just in certain contexts or situations? Are there movement impulses that you stifle or inhibit? Are there ways of moving that you'd like to cultivate or reclaim? If you could move through the world as freely as you wished, how might your movements shift? How might it feel in your body to move in this way?

5

Reshaping Body Image[1]

Due to a socialization process that leads us to make assumptions about people based on the external surface of the body rather than the content of our character, many of us struggle with body image concerns and prejudices. We are encouraged to believe that prevailing social norms about how bodies "should" look also reflect what is physically natural, psychologically healthy, and morally right. As a result, it can be easy to minimize the cost required to bring our bodies into compliance with unrealistic ideals of physical appearance and functioning. Likewise, it can be tempting to dismiss how frequently we judge the worth of others based on the degree to which they conform to prevailing body image ideals.

This chapter discusses strategies intended to provide a means for disrupting social norms of the body—not by expanding the repertoire of socially acceptable bodily expressions, but by working to disable the act of body norming itself. This disabling can be facilitated by a turn toward the lived, felt experience of the body and an intentional cultivation of the body's deep curiosity. By privileging sensation, attending to movement impulses, and honoring our embodied intuition, we access a subjective data set that informs—and potentially transforms—our relationship to objective body standards. In this way, the disruption of body norms becomes not only a strategy for resistance against oppression but a process of creative, sensual inquiry that each body engages as an ongoing liberatory praxis.

Body Norms, Body Shame, and Social Power

Patriarchy, racism, ableism, cisheteronormativity, and industrialization work together to infiltrate and occupy our body selves from the outside in (and then from the inside out) by asserting and enforcing a set of universal norms that define ideal bodily characteristics and behaviors. These body "ideals" create a narrow and tightly constricted understanding of what "normal" bodies should look and act like. All bodies that naturally (or intentionally) fall outside those norms are vulnerable to varying degrees of scorn, contempt, and abuse.

It has been argued that the more marginalized and subordinated a social position we occupy, the more we are identified as bodies, and the more pressure we experience to modify those bodies to mitigate our deviance from the norm. In other words, one way to enact oppression against members of a particular social group is to characterize them as bodily objects rather than intelligent and sentient subjects, and to simultaneously depict those bodies as uncivilized, crude, ugly, or distasteful. As the multibillion-dollar cosmetics, plastic surgery, and weight loss industries readily attest, women are prime subjects of such pressures to modify their bodies, but members of other socially disempowered and vulnerable groups are hardly exempt. The elderly are routinely encouraged to retain the appearance and functioning of their youth, while the effect of widespread and entrenched colorism supports a multibillion-dollar global market for skin-lightening products.

Of course, the cost of having a body that is considered substandard, deviant, or otherwise problematic cannot be measured in dollars alone. Body shame is a significant source of emotional and psychological distress, with consequences ranging from depression and diminished quality of life to social isolation and suicide. Body objectification and dissatisfaction are increasingly prevalent among youth, with remarkably high body dissatisfaction rates among many school-aged children. Research also suggests a high incidence of body shame among gay men, while a community-based study found that body fat dissatisfaction predicted higher rates of psychological distress, including depression and social sensitivity. Body-image concerns across other sexual minority groups encompass a wide range of issues and are inarguably salient for many within these communities.

Critical disability theorists point to the pressures to modify differently abled bodies to conform to dominant expectations of functioning and appearance, including cochlear implants for young deaf children, surgeries to lengthen limbs for people with dwarfism, and cosmetic surgery to alter the facial characteristics of people with Down syndrome. While these interventions should be open to those who want them, there is little doubt that body norms play an inevitable role in those decisions. In short, almost no one is exempt from ongoing, multiple expectations to present our bodily selves in particular ways, and this is especially true for those whose bodies fall outside dominant social norms or whose social position does not afford them the privilege of refusing to conform.

Like all social norms, we are mostly taught body norms implicitly. That is, we absorb them by watching our parents, listening to our friends and classmates, and by drinking all kinds of imagery Kool-Aid through movies, television, magazines, and social media. The bodies that are held up as beautiful and strong are the ones we unconsciously admire, and the bodies that are vilified or ignored become the bodies we learn to hate—even when those bodies look like our own. For example, in social psychology research studying the psychological effects of segregation, Black preschool children were shown two dolls that are identical except for skin color.[2] They were asked to point to the pretty doll, and then to the good doll. In response, young Black children consistently pointed to the light-skinned White doll. They were then asked to point to the doll that looks like them. As they raised their fingers to point to the brown-skinned doll, researcher Kenneth Clark described the looks of confusion, shame, and despair on their young faces as heartbreaking to witness.

As this example illustrates, even when dominant body norms harm us deeply, we often have a hard time refusing (or even recognizing) them. The visual messages about what's "okay" are so pervasive and compelling that we sometimes don't even realize we've adopted these norms as our own until they are held up for questioning. The insidious power of body norms tangles us up in a Catch-22 in which Black children are automatically disqualified from ever being pretty or good, fat women are disgusted by their own innocent flesh, and the disabled struggle to insist that their real problems are mostly ones of access rather than infirmity.

One of the ways that oppressive social systems maintain their power is by convincing the oppressed that there is something fundamentally wrong with our bodies. We are too fat, too flat-chested, too wrinkled, or too short; our skin is too dark and our hair is too curly; we use a wheelchair or a cane; our eyes are the wrong shape or color. The list of our "faults" is endless, and the work of managing, correcting, and hiding them can be exhausting and demoralizing. I'm not suggesting that we always find ourselves in a body that fits who we are, or that we shouldn't make changes to our bodily appearance. What I am suggesting is that body shame is a tool of oppression. Finding ways to radicalize and reclaim our body image serves our liberation. Cultivating our sensuality, interrogating our nonverbal communication, and reclaiming our own freedom of movement can also serve as effective strategies in resisting the deadening and demoralizing effects of body shame.

Of course, even with the vast array of body technologies currently available to us, not all bodily features can be modified. Those whose bodies place them irrevocably outside social norms for whatever reason, such as skin color, anatomical structure, or physiological functioning, have fewer ways to comply with social imperatives of body image, as do those whose limited resources do not afford them the time and money for high-status clothes, grooming, surgeries, exercise, and diet. Although there is pleasure to be found in the creative process of expressing ourselves (and our sociocultural locations and identifications) through our body image, the pressure to conform to a dominant set of ideals can undermine the freedom required for true self-expression.

While it can be argued that many of the body modifications we undertake feel "voluntary" to some extent, it's very difficult to untangle the external messages about body image and comportment that we absorb from the media, our family members, our peer groups, and our social institutions from those internal images and impulses about how our body wants to look or move. The complex and often unconscious motivations to pursue social ideals of embodiment are further complicated by the relative lack of power that members of oppressed groups possess to resist or refuse those ideals. Internalized racism, ableism, cis-heterosexism, and misogyny shape our bodily desires in ways that can be difficult to distinguish from our own preferences, and the consequences of deviance from certain body norms, such as those governing gender expression, can sometimes be fatal.

Not only is compliance enforced within remarkably narrow parameters, body norms themselves are a moving target. A quick review of the cross-cultural history of body modification reveals that opinions about bodily practices can and do vary over time. For example, within the last century in North America both men and women have come to regard unshaven armpits as slovenly and unkempt in women but not in men, even though we have plenty of historical examples to the contrary and may even understand that our disgust is not a rational response. Tattoos offer another example of the shifting ideals of bodily appearance. Today, many people mark their bodies with these permanent images as a form of positive self-expression, while only a generation ago tattoos were considered so outside the norm that they were diagnostic of certain psychopathologies.

In other words, "acceptable" bodily expression varies so widely across cultures and generations that any claims about bodies based on the presumed universality, stability, or moral authority of body norms are inherently suspect. Queer theorist Nikki Sullivan points out that the degree to which body modification is considered a viable opportunity for people to "feel more at home in their bodies" or a "monstrous" act of self-mutilation depends largely upon the social and theoretical position of the viewer.[3]

Many of us engage in practices that impair basic body functions such as breathing, swallowing, and walking (for example, by wearing ties, girdles, bras, and high heels), and some of us create permanent alterations in body structure through cosmetic surgery, circumcision, and ear piercing, for example. We alter our gaits, restrict our bodily expression, and discipline our shapes. These practices are frequently understood as normal and benign when they help our bodies to conform to desired social norms, but when similar practices are employed to transgress prevailing body norms through tattoos, scarification, chest binding, or gender affirmation surgery, for example, others can see them as excessive or pathological.

Given the fluidity, complexity, and contingency of bodily appearance and conduct in signifying social power and shaping identity, how do members of socially subordinated groups reclaim some authority over their body image in the process of liberation and empowerment? As subjects whose very identities are (at least in part) socially constructed, how do we interrogate and illuminate the choices, compromises, and creative impulses involved in shaping our body in particular ways? How do we understand questions of agency and intent in the ongoing transformations of our body selves? As we expand the range of our own bodily expressions to include representations that may have been prohibited or censured by the social worlds in which we live, how do we avoid the danger of advancing those countercultural expressions such that they become the new norms that others are expected to emulate? In exploring these questions, two analytical/methodological tools may be useful: queer theory and somatics.

Queering the Body

Queer theory, emerging out of the scholarly study of gay and lesbian identities in the 1990s, can be understood as an investigative strategy that questions normative assumptions about identity and relationality. David Halperin asserts that "queer is, by definition, whatever is at odds with the normal, the legitimate, the dominant. There is nothing in particular to which it necessarily refers. It is an identity without an essence. 'Queer' then, demarcates not a positivity but a positionality vis-à-vis the normative."[4] Applied to body norms, queer theory asks us to question how these norms came to exist and by whose authority they are enforced; it requires us to ponder how our bodies are shaped by the expectations of others, and it urges us to consider the relational implications of bodily conformity and nonconformity. If body norms are understood as the unwritten rules that govern bodily behavior and appearance in certain social settings, then how might we go about rewriting (or even erasing) these rules?

Queer theory offers a promising conceptual tool we can use in this task. For example, drawing on queer theory's roots in poststructuralist and constructivist perspectives, it becomes possible to shift our understanding of the body from an unchanging object to a series of multiple processes and unstable positions. Queering the body means shifting it from being a noun to being a verb; a body is not something one *is,* but something one *does.* And if bodies are (at least in part) processes and acts we perform, then so are body norms. By extension, if body norms are the product of reiterative acts of norming, they can be undone.

EMBODIED REFLECTION AND INTEGRATION
Making Body Norms More Explicit

Think of something you do every day that affects how your body looks or behaves. Perhaps you brush your teeth before bed, cover your hair before you go outside, or wear a necktie to work. Maybe you remove your shoes when you enter someone's home, apply lipstick after a meal, or shave your facial hair. Do you perform these body acts automatically, without thinking? What would it feel like not to do them? How might not doing these acts affect your body image? Your self-image? How do you think others would respond to you not performing these actions? What do you think of other people who don't do these things? As you reflect on your answers to these questions, use this opportunity to notice the implicit assumptions that undergird your bodily habits. Notice how social power—particularly the power to coerce, refuse, patrol, and censure—might be embedded in each of these actions.

In questioning the reproduction of body norms through our everyday actions, it is important to keep in mind that body norms, like other social norms, are not inherently harmful. Norms establish a coherent set of expectations about our roles as members of particular social groups. They can enhance feelings of group membership, support group cohesion and productivity, and help us identify behaviors that might threaten the group's safety and stability. However, norms are also equally effective at prohibiting benign differences, stifling creative dissent, inducing shame and resentment, and perpetuating inequity within and across groups.

Even within subcultures whose members denounce the inequities of the dominant culture, body norms can perform both affirming/including and restrictive/excluding functions. For example, in her blog post "On Queer Aesthetics and Not Feeling Queer Enough," Emma Hardy describes how someone once introduced her to others at a radical queer house party as "the token straight girl," even though Emma herself identifies as queer. In unpacking this overt dismissal of her sexual identity, Emma notes, "I wonder how much of it comes down to pure aesthetics. While I'm all for non-normative relationship structures, I don't look radical. I work in a corporate setting and dress the part. Apart from some bleach and a little underarm hair, I'm repellingly mainstream."

She goes on to argue that "conforming to gendered stereotypes or normative standards of beauty doesn't make me more or less queer" and asserts that "when we reduce our identities down to an aesthetic, as liberating as that aesthetic may be, we also risk commodifying it."[5] Queer theorist Nikki Sullivan concurs. She notes that within some queer and feminist communities, "the assumption seems to be that those forms of body modification that do not *explicitly* set themselves up in opposition to so-called 'normative' ideals . . . are politically suspect."[6]

The irony these stories point out—that members of oppressed social groups are perfectly capable of being oppressive about body norms within their own communities—underscores the real value of queer theory in the project of disabling body norms. Queering the body is not necessarily about altering one's appearance and behavior in defiance of dominant norms (although there's nothing wrong with that). It's about questioning our choices—or lack thereof—with respect to how our bodies look and move, regardless of our position(s) on the multiple spectrums of social identifications.

Querying the Body

The second useful tool in our project of interrogating body norms is somatic theory and practice. Somatic practices work to cultivate sensory awareness both interoceptively and intercorporeally; they draw upon what we feel in our bodies as well as what we experience in the body-to-body relational field. In other words, although body norms focus on how our bodies look and move as observed from the outside, a somatic perspective privileges how we experience our bodily selves from the inside. This shift in focus allows us to *incorporate*—literally, to take into our bodies—how it feels to enact particular body expressions. As any seasoned somatic practitioner will attest, feeling into the body in this way usually works best when approached with gentle curiosity and without a strict agenda. This attitude of inquiry allows for the emergence of sensory and imaginal data that might otherwise be overlooked.

EMBODIED REFLECTION AND INTEGRATION
Feeling into Body Norms

Think about a body norm that you enact on a regular basis. Perhaps you sit with your knees held closely together while riding on public transit, or you whiten your teeth. Maybe you wear a bra or a suit, smile at strangers on the street, remove the hair from a particular area of your body, or take medication for acne. The next time you enact this norm, notice the (perhaps subtle) bodily sensations, emotions, and images that attend this activity. See if you can suspend interpretation of this somatic data long enough to allow this new information to settle into patterns and possible understandings on its own, without imposing meaning or judgement.

By asking questions about body norms, we interrupt the automaticity of our actions and gestures. We make them less unconscious, less involuntary, and more available for possible change. To be clear, I am not suggesting that querying normative bodily expression reduces the risks associated with transgressing those norms. However, by asking ourselves how we feel in our bodies when we enact a body norm, we introduce information that was not available to us previously—information that might shift how we understand our bodily behaviors, preferences, and assumptions.

These somatic inquiries are likely to surface a range of complex responses that don't necessarily suggest a clear and simple course of action. For example, querying the established Western body norm for adult women to wear a bra might reveal uncomfortable sensations of breathing constriction and tissue compression as well as comfortable feelings of support and containment. Experimenting with transgressing the norm (in this case, appearing in public without a bra) might result in bodily sensations of freedom and mobility as well as lack of protection and an increase in feelings of scrutiny or exposure. Everyone will experience sensations and emotions unique to them, and we can use this interoceptive, proprioceptive, and socioemotional data in support of a whole range of possible actions. The point of somatic inquiry is not to collect body-centered evidence in support of predetermined change, but to enhance our whole-person awareness of self and others. In many cases, simply allowing ourselves an opportunity to be immersed in sensation without judgment or agenda can be a liberatory experience.

EMBODIED REFLECTION AND INTEGRATION
Shifting Body Norms

Feel into a body practice that you'd like to shift or a body image you're considering modifying. As you contemplate the change, ask yourself if you're fixing a "problem" or disguising a "flaw." Are you feeling pushed or drawn?

Anxious or excited? Is the desired body image coming at you from the outside or emerging from within? What would your body do if it could do anything? How might this new body expression support the cultivation of a body image that feels authentic, creative, poetic, or empowering?

BODY STORIES
Externalizing Body-Image Norms[7]

During a weekend workshop on oppression and body image, I asked participants to reflect on how their feelings and attitudes toward their own body have been shaped by the social norms and expectations they encounter from their peers, family members, and communities. Through a guided interoception exercise, I helped to facilitate the gathering of an overall felt sense of the issues and concerns they held with respect to their own body image. Then I asked them to allow an internal symbolic image to emerge that captured, for them, the essence of that concern. Rather than asking them to describe or draw that image, I instead asked participants to bring that image in the form of an object to class the following day. The next morning, as the group members were sharing their body-image objects with one another, three of them stood out.

A tall, slim young man brought a toothpick. He explained that he had been bullied as a child for being tall and skinny and that his schoolmates would taunt him with the nickname "Toothpick." An older Asian American woman brought a kimono and told the group she was struggling with the traditional gender presentation that her family members expected of her. In particular, she noted how the kimono restricted her body movements and made it hard for her to breathe. Although she did not wear a kimono in her everyday life, it symbolized for her the bodily comportment she felt she was expected to emulate. And a young Middle Eastern woman brought a shaving razor. Placing the razor in front of her, she confided to the group that she shaved her face every day to remove the visible beard and mustache that grew there. The razor symbolized for her both the hairless feminine body ideals of the North American culture into which she had immigrated and her means of assimilation.

Having group members externalize and (literally) objectify an internalized body norm can make it easier for them to recognize the source of their body shame as something that originated outside of themselves, within social and cultural contexts that are laden with power. It can also facilitate the creative exploration of that body norm in ways that allow it to transform. In most of the cases I have witnessed, that transformation does not entail an outright rejection of the body norm, such as snapping the toothpick, shredding the kimono, or throwing away the razor. Rather, the transformation takes place in more subtle and inventive ways. In this example, I asked group members to consider how their body-image object might transform by asking their body what it needed to feel more okay about this whole "body image" thing.

In the case of the young man, he reported that his internalized toothpick image had become a sapling, with roots that grew into the ground, a trunk that supported his spine, and branches that were still small but beginning to spread out. He noted with some humor that if he was going to be made of wood, at least he could be living wood. The woman with the kimono reached forward and loosened the *obi* (the wide panel of fabric that wraps around the waist of the kimono when it is worn). She stated that she was still going to wear the (symbolic) kimono, but she also wanted to be able to breathe. And the young woman with the razor decided to pass it around the circle, allowing each group member to hold it in turn. She hasn't yet made up her mind whether she is going to continue to remove her facial hair, but she remarked that the most painful aspect of this issue for her was the secrecy that surrounded it. Now when she holds her razor while shaving, she can imagine the imprint of those other hands and remember the support and understanding she felt from her group.

In each case, participants identified a source of pain connected to an internalized body norm—a belief about the body that originates from outside the self but is taken into the self, even when it causes pain. In choosing an external object to symbolize the body norm, they reexternalized it, making it available for reflection and critique by themselves and others.

BODY STORY
The Eternal Quest for a Good Queer Haircut

Imagine that you're me when I'm three weeks overdue for a haircut. In this story, my life has been hectic with travel and work, and I've let things slide. When you wear your hair as short as I do (rarely longer than an inch), three weeks is a long time. When I'm three weeks overdue for a haricut, my hair sticks out in strange places and falls flat in others. The back of my neck is uncomfortably fuzzy. My bangs are doing that weird cowlick thing again. As soon as a spare moment opens up, I call to make an appointment for a haircut.

Only to discover that my regular barber has suddenly quit her post at the local barber shop, and no one can tell me where she's gone. I alternate between concern for her well-being (Is she sick? Are her kids okay?), feelings of abandonment (Did she move away without telling me? Has she opened a shop of her own?), and bouts of panic and despair. It took me nearly a year to find this barber. She is wonderful. How will I ever find someone to replace her?

This degree of emotionality in response to a change in grooming service personnel might be considered symptomatic of an anxiety disorder or per-haps suggestive of some underlying attachment issues. In my case, however, my reaction is entirely warranted. Permit me to elaborate.

When I was twenty, I decided to get my hair cut really short. This decision was prompted both by a growing sense of androgyny with respect to my gender identity and by an unusually hot and humid summer. One day, the lank strands of damp hair clinging to my face on the long bus ride home from work finally wore away at the last vestiges of gender role conformity until they snapped. That weekend, I walked down to my local hair salon and asked for a haircut. When I showed them with my fingers how short I wanted it, they shook their heads and suggested the barber shop across the street.

The barber shop was squeezed into a tiny space between a bank and a grocery store and was appropriately called The Little Barber Shop. Inside, Frank and Rocco were stationed next to two chairs in an otherwise empty shop. After a moment of obvious confusion—*You're here for a haircut? Are you sure?*—Frank motioned me over to his chair and began to work. It took three tries before he got it as short as I wanted. But he took it down to the half inch I asked for, and I left feeling happy and free, lighter than air. When I got home, my roommates oohed and aahed, and then took turns feeling my head. My newly shorn hair was baby-soft, and as I ran my hands through it, I felt myself relaxing, breathing more deeply. I never looked back.

Frank cut my hair for seven bucks, not including tip, for as long as I lived in the neighborhood. Since then, however, getting my hair cut has not been as simple as it was that hot summer day so many years ago. For example, I have had my hair cut quickly and sloppily by barbers who seemed uncomfortable with the presence of a visibly female body in the all-male sanctum of their barber shop. I guess they figured that if they gave me a really bad cut, I wouldn't come back. (They were right.) I have had barbers come on to me, and I have been charged more than the male customers for the same haircut by the same barber. I have been leered at by (male) customers, I have been kept waiting until all the other (male) customers had been served, and I have walked into busy barber shops to be greeted by a sudden stony silence. One rainy day in Scotland, I was refused service by a shop full of barbers hanging around with no other customers in sight.

Of course, I have explored other options over the years. Every time I moved someplace new, I would ask the first queer woman whose short hair I liked where she got her hair cut. Invariably, she would name a punk boutique salon in a part of town where haircuts started at five times the cost of a barbershop cut. Or she would tell me that her partner cut her hair. I've gone to the bargain salons, with predictably unpredictable results. I've invested in electric clippers and tried cutting my own hair at home, also with patchy results. Cutting short hair well is harder than it looks.

The best queer haircut I ever got was free. I met a fellow in a bar, and he asked me if I wanted to do some demonstration modeling for a hair salon training school. Ordinarily, I would have greeted this offer with healthy skepticism, but I happened to be between barbers at the time and was feeling a bit desperate. The following week, I sat down in Billy's chair facing a room full of attentive hairdressing students, and he asked if there was anything I would not be comfortable with him doing. I told him I couldn't think of anything. He began working away with a pair of scissors, and I watched the faces of his students as they followed his every move. At one point, Billy flattened my bangs tight to my scalp with his hand and positioned his shears at the very top of my hairline. He took one, long decisive *snick*, and the whole room gasped. It wasn't until he was finished the cut and he swiveled me around to face the mirror that I could see what he'd done. My bangs were completely gone. Somehow, Billy had intuited that not only did I not want to be a girl, but I also didn't want to be living in the twentieth century. He gave me a haircut that made me look like a cross between Joan of Arc and a medieval monk. I was thrilled.

My reaction (and the contrasting reaction of the astonished/horrified hair-dressing students) brings me to a point about queerness and body image that feels important to consider. For me, being queer is not only about gender or sexual orientation. More deeply, it's about disrupting norms and expectations across a whole range of social categories. Billy's haircut tapped into something profoundly affirming about how I wanted to look in the world. It helped me realize that cutting my hair "like a boy" was only part of the disruption I needed to embody in order to feel like myself. But for some reason, the "monk cut" (as I came to call it) was unusually disturbing to people, including many queer folks. For weeks afterwards, friends and acquaintances would ask how I could ever have permitted someone to cut off my bangs. They wondered if my part-ner liked the haircut. They wanted to know what the people at work thought about my hair. This wasn't just about gender presentation; there was some-thing else going on here entirely. And it wasn't until my bangs were gone that I understood how crucial they were to current norms of human attractiveness and appropriateness.

A second point I'd like to make about queerness and hair has to do with the privileging of the visual sense in our understanding of queer bodies. Although a haircut might ordinarily be understood to fall within the bounds of body image—that is, how we manipulate the surface of our body to create a certain image for others to read—for me that manipulation has as much to do with eliciting a particular sensory experience as with the visual effects of groom-ing. For example, I wear my hair short not just because I like how it looks, but because I love how it feels. When I run my hands through my freshly shorn hair and feel the exposed contours of my neck, temples, and ears, I experience an exhilaration of freedom that is a decidedly sensual experience. One of the remarkable effects of the monk cut was how the complete bareness of my face made me feel naked to the world, in a good way. When we contemplate how we queer our bodies, it might be useful to consider that queering how they *feel* might be even more disruptive, subversive, and transformative than queering how they *look*.

So, what does this mean for embodied activism? My own experiences in the still-very-gendered world of barber shops suggest that the creation of grooming resources for the gender nonconforming might serve a real social need. I think about the trepidation I feel in trying to find a new barber, walking blind into yet another barber shop, and I can only imagine that I am not alone. Are there safe and affordable places for transwomen to get their hair done? Where do genderqueer kids get a haircut? Are they treated with compassion and respect? When we encounter someone who never cuts their hair, or who styles it in a unique way, have we considered their somatic experience in the choices they have made?

Querying the Bodies of Others

Poststructural theories of the body typically consider the body as a text onto which dominant social conventions and understandings are inscribed, and from which one's social position can be read. Indeed, some poststructural theorists argue that the body is less a material object than an effect of discourse (i.e., what we say about it). Regardless of the degree to which you understand the body as a natural, physical entity or how much you consider it a social construction, it's clear that we read onto bodies—our own and others—a vast array of cultural meanings. Nonverbal communication researchers and critical embodiment theorists have described the myriad, complex, and subtle distinctions in bodily appearance and behavior, and they have documented how social power and position are inferred and perpetuated through these body-based indicators. Through our socialization in families and groups, we learn to be as highly skilled at applying social norms to the bodies of others as we are at norming our own.

A class exercise I conduct with my graduate students asks them to read my body for indicators of my social identifications and locations. They pay attention to my posture, gait, gestures, clothes, grooming, and facial expressions, and from these observations they make remarkably astute inferences about my gender identity, social class, sexual orientation, ethnicity, age, and religion. In unpacking the exercise, I encourage students to reflect on several points: 1) the automatic ease of their reading of my body (in other words, they had read my body well before I asked them to—often within seconds of first meeting me); 2) the initial discomfort they experienced in being asked to make their assumptions about me explicit (this speaks not only to the power imbalance between teacher and student, but also to cultural prohibitions against noticing and naming the body); and 3) the high degree of interrater reliability across members of the same social group. For example, queer students were often able to read indicators of my queerness with a greater degree of specificity and nuance and tended to agree with one another about the meaning of those indicators.

Although this exercise is not about the imposition of body norms per se, it does highlight the degree to which we compare observed bodily indicators with internalized social categories, and it demonstrates that we pay attention to the social categories that are most important to us. Once students are comfortable with the idea of body reading as ubiquitous and spontaneous, they are then able to take the next step: realizing that these readings have judgments attached and that we assess people's social worth (at least in part) based on the degree to which their bodies meet the norms we have internalized.

EMBODIED REFLECTION AND INTEGRATION
Reading the Bodies of Others

Consider how you apply your own body norms to the bodies of others. How does the appearance and behavior of someone's body affect the assumptions you make about their intelligence, competence, and character? What do you find revolting, abhorrent, or ridiculous about the bodies of other people? For example, are there certain bodies (or body parts) you would feel uncomfortable touching? Rather than taking your visceral reaction to someone's body as proof of its basic unacceptability, use it as an invitation to explore your own cultural and historical relationship with the norm their body seems to transgress.

Given the habitual and largely unconscious nature of social categorization processes—and, by extension, most body norming—it can be difficult to interrupt the process long enough to interrogate or problematize the assumptions we make about people based on their body. However, recognizing that body norming is a culturally bound and subjective process (rather than assuming that body norms represent a fixed and objective truth about bodies) is an important first step. From there, exploring the problematic assumptions and assessments we make about our own bodies can serve as a methodological foundation for extending that curiosity and compassion to others.

Queering/querying the lived experience of the body in the world means not only exploring the embodied lives of those whose identifications have pushed them to the margins of the social world; it also means questioning normative assumptions about all bodies and all experience. Practically speaking, queer theory and somatic practice provide a means for interrogating body norms in ways that offer the potential for disrupting implicit assumptions about what bodies are—as well as how they should look and behave—while simultaneously anchoring our own bodily expressions in subjective sensory data. By infusing a somatic approach with the insights offered by queer theory, it becomes possible to understand that the lived, felt experience of the body in the world is never politically neutral. In other words, we can queer/query body norms not by looking at our bodies from the outside and making politically strategic adjustments, but by feeling into them, individually and collectively.

What to Wear to the Revolution: Clothing as Activism

Like the body itself, the clothes we wear communicate powerful nonverbal messages whose codes vary across time and culture. As with other mediums of communication, these messages may be interpreted (or misinterpreted) in terms of a range of social identifications and affiliations. The relationship between clothing, power, and social identity has evolved into attire with myriad and nuanced forms. From the length of a sleeve to the shape of a hat, the clothes we wear signal our place in a complex and changing social world. Although not everyone is equally attuned to these sartorial signals, they can serve as compelling markers of identity. Ask a teenager why they wouldn't be caught dead wearing *that* brand of jeans, or a

Muslim woman why they refuse to remove their burqa for a passport photograph, or an Italian widow why she wears black, and you have some idea of the power of clothing as object communication in the lexicon of the body.

The normative expectations that attach to these garments can be strictly, even violently, enforced. In ancient Greece and Rome, as well as in Europe. during the Middle Ages, strict laws dictated the colors and types of clothing that could be worn by certain individuals, and they provided a highly visible way to mark the body according to rank and privilege. For example, in Rome the color purple could only be worn by the Roman emperor and his senators, on penalty of death. In the Middle East, Islamic law dictated the length of robes (nothing dragging on the ground) and type of fabric (no silk garments) for men, while women were expected to keep their hair covered. In ancient China and Japan, the so-called "sumptuary laws" were perhaps even more detailed and restrictive in specifying the types of clothing and ornamentation that could be worn.

Even after the sumptuary laws were revoked, many societies continued to employ clothing as a means of maintaining social stratification based on class. Sociologists argue that before the twentieth century, dressing for status provided an effective mechanism for maintaining class boundaries, because the typically restrictive design of high-status clothing prevented the wearer from engaging in manual labor and required the assistance of servants to dress the wearer and maintain the garments. The design of women's clothing continues to serve a very similar purpose with respect to gender difference, consistently emphasizing ornamentality over functionality.

Clothing has also been used to destroy cultures, not just divide and stratify them. By legally prohibiting the wearing of garments associated with a particular culture, invading forces can undermine the sense of pride, identity, and belonging that traditional dress symbolizes. For example, following the Jacobite uprisings, the English forbade Scottish people to wear kilts or clan tartans. In Canada, Native dress (along with Native language) was forbidden to Indigenous First Nations children, who were forced to attend residential schools as part of their indoctrination into White settler-colonial culture.

Racist discrimination based on clothing also found expression in the Zoot Suit Riots in Los Angeles, California, during World War II. The "zoot suit"— a style of men's suit noted for its baggy pants and long jackets with wide shoulders—was popularized in the late 1930s in Harlem jazz clubs and was widely adopted by Black, Latino, and Filipino American youth. This manner of attire represented a developing artistic subculture while conveying important political meaning as well. The distinctive voluminous silhouette and flashy colors of the zoot suit represented a defiant counterpoint to the drab, somber lifestyle associated with widespread poverty among Black and immigrant communities.

However, this exuberant expression of culture challenged social norms at a time when fabric was rationed due to the war effort. In 1942, the War Production Board banned the zoot suit as a waste of fabric. Consequently, it was increasingly viewed as un-American by supporters of the war effort. At the height of the so-called Zoot Suit Riots in the summer of 1943, thousands of White American military servicemen roamed the streets of downtown Los Angeles, attacking anyone seen wearing a zoot suit. Sometimes they would violently tear the clothes off the young men wearing them before urinating on the suits or burning them in the street.

Clothing as a form of political dissent has a long and vibrant history, from Gandhi's boycott of British textiles to the berets of the French Resistance. Amelia Bloomer, an early American women's rights activist, published a newspaper called *The Lily* in which she advocated for less restrictive dress standards for women that would allow more freedom of movement than the tight corsets, petticoats, and bustles that were the norm in the 1850s. Accordingly, she became associated with the loose, gathered pants we now know as *bloomers.* A hundred years later, women in the West continued to employ clothing as a symbol of female empowerment, first by wearing trousers previously reserved exclusively for men and then by adopting the miniskirt as an expression of sexual liberation. At the 1968 Miss America pageant, women's liberation protesters demonstrated against their oppression by dumping restrictive undergarments—bras, stockings, and girdles—into a "freedom" trash can. By the mid-1970s, many young American women were going braless and bare-legged.

Less restrictive clothing is not always the chosen form of political expression, however. One of the strategies of the early civil rights movement in the United States was to dress formally and impeccably in "Sunday best" for protests, deliberately conveying an image that ran counter to many White people's preconceived notions of Black people as poor and unkempt. Later in the movement, however, younger civil rights activists reclaimed the denim of their rural slave ancestors to make a statement about class and respectability politics.

Members of the queer and trans community often use clothing to transgress social norms, as well as to signal membership in various LGBTQIA+ subcultures. Although not all of these sartorial statements should be viewed as forms of protest—sometimes they are better understood as expressions of authenticity— they effectively function to disrupt mainstream conventions about gender-appropriate attire and grooming. By choosing to wear garments typically assigned to another gender or refusing to stay within a single gender expression, queer and trans folks expose the rigidity of gender norms and make visible a complex spectrum of human identities, affiliations, and desires through what they wear. Of course, these coded expressions are not without risk, and the decision about how to dress in any given context should always be a choice that takes personal safety into account.

Sometimes, clothing is less symbolic and more literal in terms of how it functions as a tool for social change. These days, one of the most ubiquitous items of clothing worn as social protest is the T-shirt. Since the mid-1960s, T-shirts have been a popular and inexpensive medium for conveying a political message because they can be quickly and easily mass-produced and distributed. Emblazoned with quotes, statements, the names of organizations, or images of well-known figures in the movement, T-shirts are often worn during protests to promote group cohesion and establish safety. These same T-shirts are also worn on an everyday basis to signal alignment with a cause. Increasingly, T-shirts are being used for fundraising, with shirt designers donating the proceeds from sales of the T-shirt to organizations in support of a cause.

EMBODIED REFLECTION AND INTEGRATION
Are We What We Wear?

Think about a favorite article of clothing, past or present. Perhaps draw a picture of it, or you could find or take a photo of it. Recall its characteristics in as much detail as you can: color, texture, shape, cut, and fit. Consider its provenance and history: Did someone make or give it to you, or did you make or acquire it yourself? What was happening in your life when you wore this piece of clothing? Who was with you at the time? What feelings arise as you notice all the associations this piece of clothing has for you? Take a moment just to soak that all in. Then consider how that piece of clothing reflects a part of who you are. What does it say about what you value, or which social groups you belong to? What does it communicate about how you want to be seen in the world? How did other people respond to that piece of clothing when you wore it? Were they affirming or critical? How did their reaction affect how you felt when you wore it?

Now, think about a piece of clothing that you do not (or, if you no longer wear it, did not) like wearing. Maybe it was something you were required to wear or wore at a time in your life when you didn't feel as though you could make free choices about how you expressed yourself. What about that clothing felt wrong or uncomfortable for you? What did it symbolize that you innately or explicitly resisted or rejected? What cultural, social, or political statements or imperatives were woven into that article of clothing for you?

Finally, is there a piece of clothing or a way of dressing that you would love to adopt but that has felt off-limits in some way? How do you feel in your body when you imagine dressing that way? What stops you from doing it? What conditions would need to be in place for you to feel safe, comfortable, or empowered to dress this way? What normative expectations would wearing this item of clothing disrupt?

BODY STORY
My Queer Sweater

The first time my friend Diane Israel and I got together to compare notes on clothes and queerness, we began by talking about the designers and clothing lines we loved, as a way to establish some shared points of interest and reference. About halfway through the conversation, she pointed to the sweater she was wearing and noted how much she loved it, despite the fact that it was ratty and pilling and there were large holes under the arms. She confessed her love for this sweater with an apologetic tone, as if it were decidedly uncool and unfashionable to feel such affection for something so plain.

In response to Diane's tentative confession, I leapt from my chair, ran to my closet, and pulled out a sweater that bore an uncanny resemblance to the one she was wearing. It was an old, shrunken, moth-eaten cashmere V-neck in a color that could best be described as "dirt." The hem was raw and uneven from where I had shortened it with a pair of kitchen shears, and the cuffs were quietly unraveling. I told her that I loved this sweater, I loved it more than anything else in my closet, and that every time I wore it, it never failed to help me feel like myself. Diane looked at me, and we smiled at each other as only coconspirators can.

I found that garment, my queer sweater, several years ago in a dusty, cobwebby heap behind an armchair in the spare bedroom at my best friend's house. (My best friend is a clothes horse. Although he wouldn't describe himself as fashion-conscious, he has a keen eye for a piece of vintage Issey Miyake at the local Goodwill and owns upward of seventy-five T-shirts.) Suspecting that the sweater had been there for years, abandoned and alone, I rescued it from behind the chair, shook it out, and gave it a bath. It cleaned up quite nicely. Although it was riddled with moth holes, it was fully fashioned—the seams were shaped and knitted together, rather than cut and sewn—and the cashmere was a fine, soft Scottish single-ply. I asked my friend if I could take the sweater home and make it mine, and he agreed that I could. Back at my place, I cut the bottom off and cropped it to fall just under my breasts. I don't like how most sweaters hang on me, and the original menswear styling of this one had made me look like a sack of potatoes tied in the middle when I first tried it on. Cropped, however? It was nothing short of divine.

Although I could tell you many fine things about this sweater of mine—how it's soft and warm, how it breathes, how it fits over other clothing without being bulky, how it moves with me without binding or chafing, how its neutral shade complements my hair and skin color—what I want to talk about here is its queerness. This sweater's queerness is the key to my attachment to it, and my attachment to this sweater is key to my queerness.

The sweater's queerness hinges on several aspects: 1) it's a classic "men's" sweater, and my body is usually read as female; 2) I received it at least third hand, and it has already lived much of its life on the margins; 3) it's been altered and has survived; and 4) its battered, raw ugliness subverts the idea that the only clothes worthy of admiration are beautiful, new, and expensive.

The first point—that clothing offers a strategy for subverting binary gender norms—has already been articulated elsewhere more skillfully and thoroughly than I can hope to do here. The second point—that second-hand, recycled, or upcycled clothing offers a strategy for subverting capitalist norms of consumption—is one I'd like to be considered more thoroughly within activist communities. In fact, I would argue that a failure to challenge the assumptions of consumer culture when we make choices about how to represent our identities through our clothes leaves an important stone unturned. Buying and wearing new clothes is an assumption not only of class and socioeconomic privilege but also of human privilege in a more-than-human world environment that suffers as a result of our capitalist consumer choices. My sweater reminds me that it is possible to queer those norms, and to understand the value of my clothes in terms of their ecological soundness, personal and cultural provenance, and financial humility.

Cropping my sweater was another way to queer it. During the years I worked in the fashion world, first as a retail clerk and then as a window dresser and clothing buyer for a small boutique, I was often bemused at the widespread consumer reluctance to alter, adapt, or repurpose a finished article of clothing. Skirts were supposed to worn as skirts, and although you could send yours to a tailor to have it shortened, you were not supposed to wear it as a shawl. If you bought a blue pair of pants, they stayed blue the entire time you owned them. We tend to act as if clothes possess fixed and stable identities that are not open to being shaped or transformed by their interactions with us. Of course, queer theory suggests that identities are neither fixed nor stable and that many so-called "normal" identities really benefit from being turned inside out. For me, a pair of scissors and a box of fabric dye have been invaluable tools in my experiments to make the clothes I put on my body more truly mine and more reflective of my real needs and desires.

The last territory that my sweater queers is an aesthetic one. The narrow ideals of beauty in Western culture have often served to oppress those of us who identify as living outside the heterosexual and cisgender matrix. While these ideals are often focused on the human body, our clothing is not exempt from the imposition of these same standards. What we consider "beautiful" often equates to what is bright, shiny, new, and expensive. In contrast, the Japanese idea of *wabi-sabi* suggests that what is humble, worn, and imperfect can also be beautiful. Over time, I've come to love clothing that is wrinkled, faded, and worn. After I am drawn by its softness and comfort, it then invites me to look beyond the surface to notice the tiny points of grace hidden in its folds—the seven shades of heathered gray in a plain woolen scarf, the smell of dried grasses in a raw linen shirt, or the subtle textural variations of an unraveled seam.

Which brings me back to my attachment to this shrunken, drab, moth-holey, and deeply queer sweater. If it can be beautiful in all its humble imperfection, and valued despite its lack of pedigree, and bettered by being loved by someone, then so can I. And every time I wear it, I am reminded that being queer is not just who I am; it's how I shape the world.

6

Activism in Embodied Relationship

I am often struck by the dangerous narcissism fostered by . . . rhetoric that pays so much attention to individual self-improvement and so little to the practice of love within the context of community.[1]

—BELL HOOKS

Rehearse the future, rehearse the social order coming into being.[2]

—RUTH WILSON GILMORE

The central premise of *Embodied Activism* is that our everyday embodied relationships are the foundational building blocks for systemic change. This chapter recaps the strategies provided in earlier chapters—specifically, the cultivation of sensuality and the interrogation and transformation of body language and body-image norms—and describes their application to the development of relational skills across a range of contexts. Through explorations of intercorporeality, embodied moral courage, and how privilege is held in the body, this chapter explores how we might draw on our body's knowledge and skill to navigate complex interpersonal terrain and negotiate unjust power dynamics. Interviews with seasoned activists illuminate how these ideas can find practical application in community and organizational work. This chapter also extends the notion of embodied relationship to include our complex engagement with what David Abram describes as the more-than-human world—the plants, animals, rivers, and mountains that comprise our natural home.

Cultivating an Intercorporeal Ethos

Intercorporeality—literally, the property of being between bodies—is a notion first proposed by existential phenomenologist Maurice Merleau-Ponty, who used the term to extend the earlier concept of *intersubjectivity*. Merleau-Ponty argued that our relationships with others were not just between abstract subjects or selves, but between actual bodies. This emphasis on the bodily nature of our connections with others is now being supported by emerging research on the neurological basis of our capacity to feel another person's experience as if it were occurring in our own body.[3] Gail Weiss describes intercorporeality this way: "The experience of being embodied is never a private affair but is always mediated by our continual interactions with other human and nonhuman bodies."[4]

Intercorporeality underscores the role of social interaction in embodied experience. Not only do we have subjective bodily experiences; we also "take in" and "try on" the experiences of others through our embodied imagination. More significantly, the notion of intercorporeality suggests that becoming who we are occurs in the context of being with other living bodies. We inhabit a multi-personal field, and this field conversely inhabits us. Our actions affect others on a bodily level, and we simultaneously remain exposed to the embodied actions of others. This mutual shaping isn't always beneficial or consensual. In fact, one way to understand oppression is the use of power to influence the embodied experiences of others in ways that do not adequately consider the impact on them. And one way to understand resistance is to see it as the use of power to refuse to be shaped on a body level by those same forces.

The cultivation of an intercorporeal ethos—a commitment to the recognition that we are members of each other—can be supported by feeling into the embodied experiences of those who are different from us. For example, many activists begin their engagement with social justice by working on initiatives that bear directly on the oppression they have personally experienced. There's nothing wrong with this, and it can help us feel more connected to a community we identify with and want to help liberate. It can also feel profoundly affirming to be in a room with others whose bodies look and move like our own, especially if we often feel like the "deviant" body in many other social contexts.

However, if we understand the root of oppression as treating others as "less than human" to justify acting in our own interests, then it makes sense that an embodied activism that strives to undo the harm of divisive in-group/out-group tactics should include deep engagement with others whose bodies are different from ours. And of course, spending any amount of time in a group makes it clear that individual variations abound within them, even when there is a shared experience of being oppressed based on a particular bodily characteristic. Categories of social difference are constructed, not innate, and they are neither uniform nor monolithic.

Bringing together an intersectional analysis with an intercorporeal ethos means that each of us has some visceral understanding of how it feels to be disadvantaged as well as what it means to be privileged. If we reflect on these experiences deeply enough, we also come to realize that privilege does not make us happy (it simply makes us comfortable), and persecution does not sentence us to misery (although it does put pain and fear in our path more often). As we engage with one another around the social power dynamics embedded in many of our interpersonal interactions, it's crucial that we find some embodied empathy for one another. Every one of us has been thoughtless or insensitive; we all have holes in our understanding and gaps in our knowledge. We all know the sting of injustice.

As we navigate difference in our engagements and entanglements with one another, it is also important to be able to stay present to our own visceral selves. Being grounded and centered in our own bodily experience of living in oppressive social systems (regardless of our social identifications and locations) is an essential foundation for serving a mutual and interconnected embodied liberation. Knowing our oppression pain points and acknowledging our privilege blind spots can help us settle and focus when tempers flare, toes are being stepped on, or blame is being allocated. Likewise, learning to have difficult conversations with others without losing the connection to our own embodied, felt experience will ultimately strengthen a community instead of destabilizing it.

But these difficult conversations often require the prior cultivation of a certain degree of *somatic bandwidth:* the ability to make room for the bodily sensations, emotions, and impulses that arise when we're triggered, without letting them overwhelm us or unilaterally direct our actions. Cultivating somatic bandwidth creates space for us to be with our own feelings while it also allows us more space to be with the feelings of others, especially when our interactions are fraught with tension or loaded with old history.

This ability to *be who we are* in the face of others *being who they are* is central to the notion of embodied activism. It doesn't mean that we tolerate unacceptable behavior or let ourselves off the hook when we misuse power. Rather, it means that as humans we are inescapably wired for connection. Relationships are essential for our survival and well-being, and they are the place where social change ends and begins. Changing the oppressive dynamics that manifest in our relationships means having the courage, capacity, and tenacity to be in those relationships long enough (and honestly enough) for change to occur.

Recognizing our intercorporeality also means remembering how fragile *and* resilient our bodies are in the context of multiple and ongoing engagements with others. Cultivating an intercorporeal ethos means taking time to rest and to tend to our need to move, breathe, eat, and feel. It means offering touch, space, or nourishment when they're wanted and asking for those same things when they're needed. It means reveling in the wonder and mystery of the body as we also honor its limitations, pains, and challenges. Inhabiting our own skin with as much fullness as we desire—and working to support every body's right to do the same—is the whole point of embodied activism.

EMBODIED REFLECTION AND INTEGRATION
Cultivating Somatic Bandwidth

As you contemplate ways to expand your capacity to be with your own body in relation to other living bodies, where are your edges? Are there particular sensations or emotions that you struggle to be present with? Are there situations or interactions that are likely to trigger an unwanted visceral response or push you into a state of somatic disequilibrium? Conversely, are there emotions and sensations that feel like go-to responses or that you feel very comfortable with?

Consider the many shades and hues of our emotional responsiveness to the world: anger, sorrow, pride, love, shame, envy, delight, anxiety, peacefulness, disappointment, and surprise, to name just a few. Then there's a whole range of more nuanced sensations as well: feeling tired, grounded, rushed, spacious, impatient, or supported, for example.

- Where in your body do you feel these sensations and emotions?[5] Consider making a body map of your emotions in different colors and textures.

- Which emotions and sensations are harder for you to 1) witness in others, 2) experience in yourself, and 3) express to others?

- Where in your body do you feel barriers to pleasure and joy?

Understanding our own embodied responses to charged or challenging interactions can help us prepare for them, anticipating in advance where we might want support, space, or processing time. There's also a range of strategies and practices that can assist in processing the somatic residue of previous emotional events. Many somatic psychotherapy modalities are expressly oriented toward accessing, transforming, and releasing emotion in the body. The "Community Resources" section in chapter 7 includes several such options. It's also possible to work with uncomfortable emotions and sensations by intentionally expanding our somatic vocabulary in other ways. Dance is a powerful conduit for the bodily expression of human emotion, and many people find yoga, sports, massage, and the martial arts extremely effective in creating a more spacious container for all the feelings and sensations that life elicits.

When an uncomfortable or overwhelming bodily response to a situation occurs in the moment, to create more space for that response it can be helpful to draw on the strategies outlined in the somatic first aid kit presented in chapter 2, particularly the grounding, orienting, and comforting/connecting steps. Note that these grounding, orienting, and connecting strategies should not be considered an attempt to replace a challenging emotion, such as anger, with a more "positive" (read: socially acceptable) emotion. All our emotions—including fear and anger—have their purpose and can be used in the service of fair and principled relationships. Instead, the value in staying grounded, oriented, and connected while simultaneously in the throes of strong emotion means we're less likely to lose our heads while finding our bodies.

Of course, a little bit of somatic disequilibrium is not a bad thing; it lets us know that we're no longer in familiar territory, in a place where stretching and learning can happen. In other words, being present to our bodily sensations during our interactions with others can introduce feelings that are temporarily distressing and disorienting. An ethics of intercorporeality asks us to question (but not to discount) how we hold and orient our bodily selves in relation to the world, and these shifts are not always comfortable or easy. Staying in touch with how unbalanced or ungrounded we feel in our bodies while in relationship with others can provide important signals about whether this is an interaction we should pursue. Sometimes our somatic disequilibrium is a sign we should discontinue contact until we feel more solid, clear, and aligned.

An intercorporeal ethos is worth little unless and until it's practiced in real-life situations, where things can get messy and confusing, even when we hold the best of intentions. The embodied praxis section that follows offers some guidelines that can help us infuse our values into our engagements with others.

EMBODIED PRAXIS
Guidelines for Engagements That Embrace an Intercorporeal Ethos

To help you remember the guidelines in this section, think of the acronym VOICES, which stands for *voluntariness, owning, inquiry, congruence, equitable,* and *symphonic.*

Voluntariness

Even in the most seemingly inconsequential interactions with others, we often have an opportunity to deepen a connection, disrupt a harmful pattern, or attend more thoughtfully with our bodies. And, of course, sometimes our engagements with others are full of significance. Even in the moment, they feel like an important opportunity to make a difference, and to make things different. As we consider how we want to engage—through listening, acting, speaking, or simply observing—it's important that we also consider *whether* we want to engage. Sometimes we're just not up for it; we're tired, triggered, overwhelmed, confused, or we feel like we've been outmaneuvered or set up. Maybe this feels like the umpteenth confrontation over an old issue, or an unexpectedly fraught new dynamic.

Whatever the reason, it's important to listen to our body's signals. Is there a "yes" from somewhere deep inside—even a quiet one? Do we feel some support from within us, some capacity to bring ourselves freshly to this new engagement? In addition to our own sense of internal resourcing, do we have sufficient support from other sources? Are we willing and able to experience the other as a sensing, feeling, breathing being? Do we believe that they might also be willing to experience us as a sensing, feeling, breathing person? If so, perhaps the conditions for voluntary and consensual engagement have been met. While it's not always possible to ensure the criterion of voluntariness exists in a particular interaction—sometimes our hands are tied, for whatever reason—it's almost always a good idea to check if a mutual "yes" is present. More importantly, respecting our deep, embodied "no" helps ensure that we aren't subjecting ourselves to ongoing distress or injury just because we've been led to believe that we aren't ever permitted to refuse or walk away from an interaction.

Although having a choice about whether to engage is often key to an outcome that feels generative rather than forced, there's a flip side. Refusing to engage in a difficult interaction because we don't feel "safe enough" can be a problem when we hold a lot of privilege relative to those we're interacting with. This can happen when we're "called in" to a conversation about a problem, such as a microaggression we've enacted, or an issue we've been oblivious to because our privilege insulates us from the discomfort and distress that others are feeling. In these situations, it might be useful to ask ourselves whether we're avoiding an interaction because we're unwilling to take risks that might expose our bias and prejudice. In those cases, doing the inner work of cultivating our somatic bandwidth can help us stretch our capacities and make braver, more ethically responsive choices. What prior work do we need to do, and what support do we need in order to engage in difficult conversations while still staying connected to our embodied selves?

Owning

Once we've agreed to engage, owning our embodied experience helps keep the interaction real and personal. While it can be tempting to pull out a well-honed argument or a compelling rationale, communicating solely from the realm of theories and beliefs can compromise the authenticity and relatability of our engagement. What are we feeling and sensing? What's in our heart? What are our spine and our gut telling us? Speaking from our body, rather than always invoking some abstract analysis or universalized notion of what's happening, helps us stay human, to ourselves and to others.

The language we use can also help support owning our experience. Although how we talk about personal experience has lots of important cultural variations that need to be acknowledged and respected, it might be helpful to consider using "I" statements when describing our own thoughts, feelings, and perspectives. For example, we can say "I feel misunderstood" rather than "You don't understand"; we can say "I disagree" rather than "You're wrong." Regardless of the words we use to express ourselves to others, owning our embodied experience means admitting to ourselves the depth and breadth of our sensations, emotions, and impulses. Only then can we truly listen and respond.

Inquiry

If our bodies tell us anything, it's that experience is multifaceted, people are complex, and change is the only constant. Although we may be primed to see and feel old patterns in new situations, the present moment can unfold in unexpected ways if we let it. There's little value in engaging with others around issues of social injustice if we're only interested in proving a point. We might feel vindicated or enjoy a moment of feeling morally superior, but we likely haven't changed anything or anyone.

Instead, being curious—not just in our minds but in our bodies—can allow new openings, new perspectives, and new sensations to arise. And in that mutual arising, new patterns of engagement are formed. What might be discovered if we're willing to be with one another without assumptions? Without preconceived notions of identity? How might our bodies respond if we truly met one another with open minds and open hearts? An attitude of inquiry and curiosity—one that suspends judgement but does not neutralize values—is crucial here. Let's also ask ourselves what is silent (or being silenced) and get curious about what questions aren't being asked. An intercorporeal ethos means that while we listen to our own body, we also listen to the bodies of others.

Congruence

Engaging with others in a way that is congruent with our values means extending to them the humaneness with which we also want to be treated, opening a pathway to a more emotionally honest interaction. When we feel our values—such as integrity, fairness, compassion, and honesty—in our bodies, they seep into our words and our gestures, into the tone of our voice and the quality of our gaze. For example, feeling into the value of compassion can soften our hearts without weakening them and create an opening through which mutual understanding and respect can be generated. Feeling into our commitment to fairness might elicit a quality of steadfast resolve in our bodies while feeling into the principle of honesty might evoke an inner steeliness that supports us in speaking our truth. How do you experience your values on a body level, and how can you bring them into engagements that are transformative?

Equitable

Equity is not the same as equality. Whereas *equal* suggests an impartial, even division of the relational resources of time, space, and attention (e.g., ten minutes for you to talk and ten minutes for me to talk), an *equitable* distribution recognizes that justice is often better served when the person with the least power or the greatest need is afforded the time, space, and attention they require to feel seen and heard. Asking for (and sometimes demanding) what we need for an interaction to work for us can make a real difference. By the same token, when we come into a situation where we hold a lot of power or privilege relative to the others in the room, we might want to sit back and take up less space.

Symphonic

In keeping with the VOICES acronym for these guidelines, this last suggestion is anchored in the belief that collective transformation can only occur

when everyone's voice is heard, and that each voice will be a little different. No social group speaks with one unified, monolithic voice, and no one
person represents all members of their social group. At the same time, representation matters. In some situations, it will be fairly straightforward to
determine if everyone's voice has been heard, and in other situations it will
be virtually impossible. Despite the challenges, asking to hear from everyone who wants to speak and asking about those who might not even be in
the room is a good place to start. Asking for dissenting voices and noticing
the silences helps to create the symphony of voices needed for sustainable
change.

The following interview illustrates one way to implement an intercorporeal
ethos by drawing on a technique introduced earlier in this book. A group of psychology students used the Focusing practice (discussed in chapter 2) to develop
a way to feel into each other's differences—across social locations, identities,
and experiences—on a body level.

Focusing Together

In this interview, Niki Koumoutsos, Kaleb Sinclair, and Sean Ambrose discuss
the use of mutual Focusing to build embodied capacity for connection across
difference.

Rae: You were all in a graduate psychology program together and found that
there was something missing for you with respect to antioppression work. What
were the first impulses to look at Focusing to create an approach that was different from what you'd already encountered?

Sean: Being in a shared cohort in an intimate educational setting, we learned
a lot of very progressive theories around social justice and cultural identity. Yet
I was feeling all this top-heavy thinking and mind stuff. I remember looking at
each other from across the classroom (we usually sat in circles) and feeling a big
miss for me. In a lot of these classes, I remember thinking that we're getting all
this information and now we're going to use it to be, for lack of a better word,
"woke." Then suddenly we're in some big argument about something, and then
class is over and we leave.

We have these theoretical frameworks that are supposed to be helping us learn to better see the other, but we're missing our own embodied experience. Then we have trouble figuring out how to come back and meet each other. So, relationships are the primary focus of our project. We use Focusing as an entry point, but any form of embodied exercise that you're using in a relational, collective way should work. From our Focusing experience together, the "me" becomes part of the "us," and now I have parts of Kaleb and Niki that are gently in my body now. We take the time to create an opening to an earlier developmental space so that when Kaleb or Niki share some of their stories, I put them somewhere in my body.

It's not like I'm appropriating Kaleb's or Niki's experience or identity or anything like that. We meet at this very present space where we recognize our identities and then we just kind of let go of that and come into this embodied space where we share together. And that sharing transforms my perceptual embodied experience, which I can then take out into the world. Niki and Kaleb come with me into the classroom and into the office with my clients. Their experience inside me creates an opening for me to listen to others in a way that grounds me, so I can start listening with my body.

Niki: I think a lot of this work is informed by the onslaught of trauma, distress, and grief that was present in the world around the time we started learning Focusing. I noticed that when practicing Focusing outside class with my peers, something was happening between us. My understanding of Focusing is that it's meant to be an individual experience, but what I noticed—possibly because of being situated so closely together in a cohort in this difficult time—was that something was happening between us, for us, around us, and through each other. It wasn't just my individual thing that was happening. Something was unfolding between us. Gradually, we thought maybe there's a way we can use this to explore how we can become better listeners. How can I listen better with my whole body? How can I listen to the things that are coming up for me and at the same time also really listen and respect your experience?

One example of how our relational Focusing work together has changed things for me is with respect to my gendered experience in very heady, intellectual spaces. Typically, they shut me down. I really love the theory. I get excited about it. But in a formal classroom environment, I can feel really shut down in conversation because I don't want to compete for space or time. I'll just wait for it to be over. My experience of being in a female body and being trained to be deferential means that I usually assume that someone else is going to be louder or have stronger feelings or better thoughts. Which can be a position of a female body: I'll just wait for it to be over instead of articulating what I need. But because of our Focusing experiences together, Sean and Kaleb now invite me into the intellectual conversations. They might say, "Hey, Niki, I know we've talked about this before. Is this something you could share at a larger level?" Even seeing them do it for other people creates an invitation for me. It's a huge shift for me to be invited.

At the same time, I don't want to be *the* example of gender issues for someone else. In the paper we coauthored,[6] we note that while our identity markers are important, they're not the only piece of who we are. I'm in a colonized body. Our relationships are already colonized. It happened way before I ever got here. So that's a beautiful entry point to why Focusing was helpful: because it gave us more embodied precision in its imprecision. I don't have to have the precise, exactly right "woke" words to be engaged here. It allows for something different to occur between us.

Kaleb: I share the overall arc of what's already been said—this deeper listening that the world often falls short in attempting to do. Particularly when we are all colonized bodies and there is so much intentional difference that is put onto our beings, to stratify us in so many ways and help us not get to this proximal place. Being able to slow down and go to this deep, empathetic listening where we are in differently identifying bodies—and that's very important because there's so much knowledge and wisdom in difference—but also returning to something that's primordial, before colonization, just bodies together, plugged into this deep intimacy. Empathy is forged through proximity, so that the closer we get to people through our entire beings, the more we gain a deeper understanding. And I think for me as a BIPOC body, but also just as a human being, I need that proximity because there's so much in this world that attempts to quell hope.

In this embodied space we've been able to forge hope, really sit with the pain and struggle but also with those moments of happiness too. Happiness among the pain, finding that eye of the storm, and gaining insight into how we are in spaces when there is difference. For me, this took off when George Floyd was murdered. Being in the protests on the streets of Seattle, I remember thinking, okay, we're all here, but are we actually all connected to the same thing? That took away a lot from me. You could feel the dissonance. The space was chaotic, and there wasn't any real kind of unity. It's a weird feeling, being so physically close to someone yet so far away. I would've loved to be in the same space while being intentional about how close we get. And I think that is what this Focusing thing has been for me.

Rae: Let me see if I'm understanding this right. While there's a physical closeness that bodies can be in together, what I hear you talking about is a relational closeness that happens when people are actually in their bodies while they're sharing space. That just being in the same room together and focused on the same event or issue isn't the same as being viscerally in touch with your own embodied experience while also letting the visceral experiences of others in. What you're doing with this Focusing practice is tapping into this process of deeply touching into what's happening in your body while in the presence of someone who's doing the same. And when you do that, there's a way in which the embodied experience of the other gets inside.

Kaleb: I remember Sean saying to me, "I want to get to a place where I can tattoo my flesh with the gift of the other's embodied experience." I always carry that with me.

Rae: This is a way to let one another inside us in a way that is not appropriating their experience and not assuming anything, just because I've let a person with a particular set of social locations into the felt experience of my body. Not assuming that, just because I have someone with those social identifications in my visceral experience, I can speak from that location or have any right to that experience. Or that I now have some generalizable insight into those social identities beyond just that unique individual. What I'm hearing is that for you all, there's something about letting one another inside somatically that feels different from the usual kind of social justice work or diversity, equity, and inclusion training. That this mutual Focusing experience represents a different paradigm, a fundamentally different approach to how social change happens.

Niki: I would add that when we're also able to stay with this embodied presence while in each other's presence, there's more ability to shift away from how I'm a colonized body. It enables different things to unfold between us. It's a different quality of presence. It's a different way to join a conversation or even have a conversation. But it's not easy. When we meet to practice, we always say, "I don't want to be here, but it's worth it." That risk of vulnerability is so, so worth it. And the practice of Focusing gives me a different availability out on the street. I can do things differently. I can approach things differently.

Rae: I often describe what I think you're saying as cultivating somatic bandwidth. Like there's more room in our bodies to do something different. You can meet someone differently rather than just replaying the scripts we were socialized into.

Niki: Yes. I've expanded to try something a little different and to invite someone to be there with me. They can always decline the invitation. Absolutely. But I have more in me than I did before.

[At this point in the interview, Niki tells a story about walking her dogs recently when one of them began paying a lot of attention to a Black man parked in a car nearby. The dog was making quite a fuss, and Niki was aware of several narratives running through her brain as she tried to decide how to proceed. She was aware of the old racist script that Black men are dangerous, and she felt she should probably just move on. She was also very aware that being approached by a White woman in a residential neighborhood could feel quite dangerous for the Black man. But because of her experience of working with Focusing, she tried to invite a connection instead. She tentatively approached the car, the man rolled down his window, and they had a playful exchange about how the dogs were so determined to get closer to the car and were behaving as if they were dancing to the music coming from it.]

Sean: Niki's story is so subtle. It's the quotidian, it's the everyday, and yet this is what we're getting at.

Kaleb: Niki's story is particularly potent for me. I felt a deep emotion listening to it because of the connection and the expansion beyond what's usual.

I've used Focusing to help me really ask the question, "What's going on here and why?" Being in a male-identified body, this questioning helps me plug into how I am in different spaces, noticing that maybe I'm talking too much or maybe the power dynamic is in flux. How can I pay respect and homage to female-identified bodies and other-identified bodies that have so much knowledge and wisdom to share? And yet I'm taking up the space. Maybe they don't feel comfortable asking me to step down, and I need to be able to slow down myself and create that space, that opening.

A lot of the gifts that Sean and Niki have given me have inspired curiosity for me in ways that I couldn't have perceived. For example, I think there can be pressure in the Black community to not even attempt to understand the White experience. And I understand this, but I can't stop there. For me, working with Focusing together has created this intense curiosity and empathetic drive to create engagement with the White community in a way that I couldn't have done before. Because I didn't know how much was residing within White-bodied people when it came to these kinds of visceral conversations in their attempt to engage with Black-identifying bodies.

I dream of a world that is beyond the colonized body. Yes, we are different, but I don't want our difference to create this unreachable, unattainable place where I can't understand you because you're so different from me—that's society's message—and so I should just not even try to attempt to understand you. Really trying to hone into that and challenge it has been, I think, the biggest blessing of this Focusing group.

Rae: I'm hearing this real commitment to relationship. Not just an openness to it, but a real commitment to it.

Sean: Kaleb shared a story with us where he's walking with his White friend, and they're in a conversation, and it starts getting a little bit heavier, and their voices get a little bit louder. And when Kaleb is sharing the story with me, we're in a Focusing space. I'm fully, actively listening to him and I'm letting the receptors of my body resonate with what he's saying. And as his tone is rising, it's raising what I'm feeling. Although I'm only witnessing at this point, it's not a disconnected witnessing.

Rae: Kinesthetic, empathetic witnessing.

Sean: Exactly. We're cognizant of identity, but we're not letting that be the end of the story. When we're Focusing, all these identity things that are so subtle and yet so visceral get picked up on that space. When Kaleb opens to me by telling me that story about his friend, we're now sharing it in this communal space of relationship, and we're shifting what bonds can be. And then that experience of taking Kaleb's story inside goes into Niki's movement out in the environment where she can orient herself in a different way in space. And then she brings that story about the dogs back to me. And so what's going on here is not a linear path but a circular, relational, horizontal path with fluctuating levels. It's a very queering space, hearing my friends talk and feeling myself opening to them.

Niki has helped me discover this really grounding sphere at the bottom of my pelvic floor, and it's where we've done a lot of gender work and a lot of work on our Whiteness. It's allowing me to come a little bit closer in, and it shifts how I can hear them. Our intentionality with closeness is different here. We want to empower each other, but we're also aware that we're going to fail each other. And in that failure, we can rupture and create resilience around these tiny little subtle things. Because we know we have this sustainable place where our bond can go through the rupture. In togetherness and with compassion, the suffering of it becomes healing and empowering. I'm no longer just an individual in my little flesh suit. We're not appropriating each other's experience; I can't talk from them. But I can listen from them. And what I can listen from is the resonant experience of my friends sharing their stories of oppression and privilege and the intertwined complexity of those two things. And what that does is let me create a wider environment.

[Sean then tells a story about being at a Goodwill store and crossing paths with an interracial couple. Sean, who is White, was wearing an Angela Davis T-shirt, and the young Black man in the couple approached Sean and said, "Do you know who's on your shirt?" In that moment, Sean recognized all the complexity and potential discord in what was occurring but was also able to resist framing the encounter as an inevitable rupture in the social space. As he describes it, Sean was able to tap into the relational bonds of support formed through his Focusing work that helped him feel like he wasn't dealing with the situation all on his own. He was able to resist getting defensive and showing off his antiracism creds: *Hey, you should know I've been doing my antiracist homework, and this is Angela Davis, and let me tell you a little bit about the prison system,* and so on.]

Sean: I can have the best theory and I can give you all these LGBTQ-affirmative, Black Lives Matter–supporting statements. I can put them on my website, you know, but the truth is that until I've sat with some of these stories and let them enter my body, I can't really understand those theories. I can say them, but it's just shine.

Going straight to the theory just jumps over so much, and then we just miss each other, and we can't listen to each other. We all have a plethora of these subtle microaggressions, and instead we're attempting microauthenticity or microreparation. How do we show up in these spaces differently? I need to discern that the Black man who I passed in the Goodwill store doesn't need me to justify myself. I don't need to do that, and I can feel okay about it, because my community comes with me. And while I understand why wearing this T-shirt could be problematic, I want to respond to them from a more intimate space that is meant to empower us.

Rae: What I'm hearing across so much of what you're saying is this dynamic between recognizing, acknowledging, appreciating, and respecting difference.

Sean: Yes. It's reverence for difference.

Rae: Oppressive social systems often make difference a point of disconnection. And what I'm hearing you all say is that there is a connection within that difference. It's possible to make connections that don't erase your social locations and your history. The difference is a place where you connect from, with reverence and empathy, and compassion. Not because you feel sorry for people who have been harmed, but because you recognize that feeling in your own flesh and because you're committed to taking some experience of that harm into yourself.

Kaleb: I always use this analogy when I talk to my clients or my partner. We're told to lift this huge boulder—which is all of the oppressive spaces, all the being boxed in, being characterized and labeled—by ourselves. And we can't lift it by ourselves. It's impossible. What Focusing does is make empathy into an active form. Where I come to listen and to engage. I bring my experience, but it's not totalizing. And I'm fully open to accept your experience. And when our differences are destabilizing, we forge stability from that together. We communally come to lift this rock together. So it doesn't crush you, and it doesn't crush me.

The idea that antiracist or antioppression work is without rupture is a lie. You will rupture, but there is the possibility to create repair. It is human nature to rupture and to fail. And especially in colonized bodies, we're set up to fail. But through empathetic engagement, there is a possibility to engage in communal sharing. And that's in the active form. This dance is not something that's stagnant; it's an everpresent dance. But we have to get away from the thought that this work is comfortable. Because it's not.

Rae: And it's not something that we can do through book learning.

Kaleb: Yeah, no book does that. The embodiment piece is so important. Because if I don't know how you feel inside your body when, for example, you're called the N-word or any type of slur, I can't carry it. I don't carry it the same. It's uncomfortable to carry, but it's important that I do.

Rae: Being willing to carry someone else's experience, with the recognition that they will carry your experience. It's mutual. What I'm hearing is that that's the agreement and the commitment to relationship that we were talking about earlier: I will let your experience into my body, and I will carry it, and you will let mine in and carry it and hold it within you, and we will let that change us both.

One Thousand Paper Cuts: Understanding and Transforming Embodied Microaggressions[7]

Psychologist Chester Pierce coined the term *microaggressions* to name the subtle but cutting put-downs that Black people experience as part of their everyday experience in a racist world. The term has since proven so descriptive of stigmatized people's experiences that it has become centralized in social justice discourse, largely through the contributions of Derald Wing Sue and his colleagues. Noting that covert microaggressions sometimes have more harmful impact than overt forms of marginalization, Sue defines them as "brief, everyday exchanges that send denigrating messages to certain individuals because of their group membership."[8] These seemingly insignificant relational "paper cuts"—slights, mischaracterizations, assumptions, and oversights—are regularly inflicted onto members of socially subordinated groups and have been shown to have significant and enduring impact on our health and well-being.

While some of these microaggressions are verbal—asking a person of color where they're *really* from, persistently mispronouncing names, or using the wrong pronouns, for example—many microaggressions are enacted nonverbally. Touching a Black person's hair or a pregnant person's belly without permission, stiffening and turning slightly away when a queer couple holds hands, rolling our eyes when a colleague with a speech impediment haltingly proposes a new idea in a business meeting—these nonverbal behaviors all signal a failure to consider the other as fully deserving of dignity and respect. At the same time, many of these nonverbal microaggressions are unintentional, springing more from our privileged ignorance than from malice. Indeed, Sue argues that microaggressions possess a power to wound *because* the perpetrator often transmits them unconsciously, and because they frequently remain nebulous and difficult to articulate.

As a result, these nonverbal enactments of bias can have a profound impact on the recipient. Not only are we dealing with an offender who is oblivious to their aggression; in some cases, we may not be consciously tracking our bodily responses either, leaving us with a vague sense of being mistreated without feeling able to name or describe what happened. In other instances, we can feel understandably confused and perturbed when a verbal message that is technically free of bias is delivered in a nonverbally hostile or dismissive manner, leaving us—the recipient of the microaggression—questioning or second-guessing our perceptions. Navigating the complex and subtle territory of microaggressions requires that we become more skilled in identifying, validating, and helping to shift the damaging nonverbal patterns that occupy this silent yet meaning-laden substrate of interpersonal relations.

My research on the embodied experience of oppression has surfaced numerous instances of nonverbal microaggressions across a range of social identifications and locations. Many of these microaggressions are conveyed through posture, gesture, and facial expression. For example, in one study, research participants told my fellow researchers and I that they were highly sensitized to movements in others that signaled disapproval, dismissal, or contempt, such as crossed arms, frowns, shrugs, and cold shoulders. Participants said that in addition to learning how to scan the environment for nonverbal indicators of threat, their bodies displayed certain responses and adaptations to these hostile social worlds. One participant noted how her body movements unconsciously changed depending on her social environment:

> It depends on what culture I'm navigating through. It doesn't happen consciously, when I realize I'm tightening up or straightening up around people that I perceive as more powerful or possibly hurtful. It's only when I leave them and I feel myself unwind that I notice that I can breathe more deeply. My movement repertoire changes depending on the culture I'm in and the context of power I'm around.

This speaks to the somatic impact of living in a social world where microaggressions are common as well as to the adaptive nonverbal strategies needed to navigate these challenging environments.

In the same study, several participants noted the impact of space on their experience of oppressive interactions with others. A common theme was not feeling allowed to take up space, resulting in an overall constriction of body movement: hunched posture, limbs held close to the body, and small gestures. A female participant recalled the almost daily experience of riding the subway to work, where some men sat with their legs spread so wide that they took up room on the seats on either side. On one occasion, she constricted herself so tightly to make room for the man sitting next to her that her leg muscles began to go into spasm. Although she was fully aware of how this embodied microaggression invaded her personal space and hurt her body, she also confessed that she didn't feel safe pushing back.

Microaggressions enacted through touch figured strongly in several of our participants' narratives, providing a good illustration of asymmetrical nonverbal interactions, where individuals holding more social power are accorded "touch privileges" that are not reciprocal. One interviewee related an instance where a fellow student she didn't know particularly well came up behind her in a school computer lab and began massaging her shoulders. She was caught off guard and taken aback and told the young man that she didn't appreciate being touched in that way. The man reacted by telling her to "chill out." Immediately, the young woman felt she was wrong for having set a boundary.

In retrospect, the participant realized that the young man's outrage was likely rooted in a sense of entitlement—the feeling that he should be able to touch whomever he wanted, as long as his intentions were benign. Several participants described feeling a complete lack of choice in whether someone touches them or not. Rather than saying no, they experience an automatic muscular contraction or armoring that shields them against the felt experience of unwanted touch. One participant observed that the chronic tightness required to tolerate unwanted touch often means that even positive touch is not allowed in.

The eyes are subtle but powerful tools of communication, and many of our research participants spoke about how strongly they were affected by microaggressions involving eye contact or gaze. In the words of one participant, "I felt unwelcome in certain contexts not by what anybody said specifically but by how they looked at me . . . just their unspoken hostility that I wasn't supposed to be there, or I didn't belong, or I didn't match." Another participant described the sexist microaggressions that resulted in the development of a finely attuned sensitivity to the gaze of others:

I would be very surprised that any female walking down the street wouldn't be conscious of men watching you, and how you have to be a little bit more conscious of what you're wearing, conscious of space, those sorts of things. It's something that has oppressed me throughout my life . . . the frustration of just walking down the street and being aware of men looking at you in a way that doesn't feel comfortable.

Another participant spoke about how she avoids eye contact not to avoid seeing others, but to avoid feeling seen by others, as if by not looking she could become invisible and prevent others from seeing her fat, butch-lesbian body as different and wrong. In a world where the gaze of others was so often experienced as a microaggression—as dismissive, critical, and judging—she coped by restricting her own gaze, thereby limiting the harm that might pour in.

As this discussion of nonverbal microaggressions illustrates, our bodies are intimately connected to the transmission and reception of messages that speak volumes about the power dynamics embedded in the relationships between members of different sociocultural groups. Because bodies are the medium through which these dynamics play out, bodies also hold the memory, impact, and imprint of these exchanges.

For our research participants, these somatic effects included intrusive body memories (remembering only the interoceptive feelings or other bodily sensations of the traumatic encounter) and physiological reactivity upon exposure to cues that resembled an aspect of their oppression (feeling triggered). Nearly all of our research participants spoke about how highly sensitized and attuned they feel to the nonverbal reactions and responses of others, and it was clear that their relational sensitivity was rooted in a history of marginalizing and repressive experiences with others. One participant described a type of somatic vigilance with respect to White people and spoke about how crucial it felt to be able to read their nonverbal communication, especially when in close physical proximity. Another acknowledged that she becomes increasingly self-conscious of her bodily appearance and movements when members of a dominant social group do not respond to her nonverbal cues with some degree of kinesthetic empathy.

In describing the somatic impact of oppression, most participants spoke about a history of profound disconnection from the felt experience of their bodies. In many cases, this disconnection was something that participants had only realized recently through the process of addressing the impact of oppression. At the same time, participants also described this withdrawal from the felt experience of the body as initially functional—something that allowed them to survive the painful feelings generated by their experiences of being oppressed. However, the mechanism that served to protect them from unbearable distress also served to disconnect them from a general sense of sensory awareness. In other words, the altered state of consciousness provoked by traumatic stress is one in which we cannot experience bodily sensations fully or accurately, and this lack of connection to our physical selves may produce a range of understandably unintended consequences: distorted body image, distorted awareness of physical space boundaries, and poor movement coordination.

A conscious understanding of the nature of nonverbal communication and its involvement in the establishment and maintenance of privilege and bias can help us recognize when these somatic symptoms arise from the chronic trauma of oppression. By making the nonverbal components of our everyday relationships more conscious and available for reflection and interrogation, we can then begin to experiment with new ways of being in the world. Embodied microresistances provide a way to push back and hold our ground in the face of the constant erosion of pride, dignity, and self-respect that microaggressions produce. By refusing to enact the nonverbal scripts of subordination and reclaiming physical expressions that feel authentic and empowering, we can begin to experience our bodies as sources of personal and social power, not just as targets for discrimination and abuse. Understanding how our bodies are implicated in and affected by microaggressions also supports us in developing authentic embodied subjectivities that, through everyday embodied microresistances and microinterventions, can support macrolevel social change.

EMBODIED PRAXIS
Disarming Embodied Microaggressions

Where do the scars from your own relational paper cuts live in your body? How do they occupy your tissues, organs, muscles, and nervous system? How does the embodied memory of previous microaggressions inform how you approach new situations in similar contexts? Are you aware of bracing, holding, attacking, or withdrawing in anticipation of yet another sting or slight? How might you care for these old wounds to support new patterns of relating? As we shift our embodied experience toward decolonization and liberation, we can support that shift by developing strategies for intervening when an embodied microaggression occurs.

Some Strategies for Responding
to an Embodied Microaggression

- Whenever possible, take time for a breath or two and to connect with a sense of spacious, grounded support in your body. Find in your body the quality of attention and presence that you want to bring into the interaction, whether that's openness, patience, fierceness, or curiosity. These qualities will shine through in your movements, expressions, breathing, and tone of voice and can positively infuse the relational space between you and the other person.

- Describe the behavior (not the person) and its impact on your body. For example, "When you shrugged your shoulders just then, I felt dismissed, and my stomach tightened up." Then connect your bodily experience to the larger social justice issue. For example, "I'm concerned that your actions stem from an underlying assumption about me as a [person of color/disabled person/female-bodied person] or some unconscious privilege you hold as a [White/able-bodied/male-bodied person]." You might also express this more casually: "This feels like it's about [racism/ableism/sexism] to me."

- Be curious. If you're up for it (and if you think the person who enacted the microaggression is open to it), ask them about their experience. Were they aware of their bodily behavior? This can illuminate the often-unconscious nature of embodied microaggressions. However, inviting them to share their experience should not be considered an opportunity for them to defend, deny, or justify their behavior.

- Ask for the relational shift—not just the superficial performative action— you want from them. Depending on the nature of the microaggression and how the conversation is going, this might be an apology, an acknowledgement, making amends, or a commitment to changed behavior going forward.

- Alternately, you can engage your body as an instrument of change. This strategy allows you to intervene without words and can be a surprisingly effective way to get your power-challenging message across. For example, if the microaggression was an invasion of personal space, play with the space in ways that subvert the social norms of how space is usually shared: move in, move away, or turn around. If the microaggression took the form of a facial expression, make a face back. How you use your body will depend on a lot of factors (including safety), but using the same body-to-body communication channel rather than attempting to translate body language into words is sometimes the simplest, most effective way to respond to an embodied microaggression.

- Once the intervention is over, take some time to return to the embodied experience of feeling spacious, grounded, and supported. Debrief with a trusted friend or colleague if that feels right.

Of course, we enact microaggressions as well as being subjected to them. We all have examples of when something we've said or done has caused pain and distress in others. Between well-meaning people, these relational injuries are mostly unintentional and unconscious, arising from blind spots in our capacity to fully see and recognize the other. Although these blind spots developed through a process of socialization over which we have little control, we're still responsible for the impact our actions (and inactions) have on other people. And yet, many of us struggle to recognize the ways in which our privilege obscures the power differences that lead to hurt and harm. Even when we're committed to living in ways that are ethical and just, sometimes there's a real gap between what we believe and how we show up in the world.

How might unconscious bias and privilege live in your nonverbal patterns of communicating with others? Notice how you interact nonverbally with others and how you might unconsciously use space, touch, posture, and gesture to signal power or status. Take seriously the embodied microaggressions that others point out to you. One of the cornerstones of relational repair is the process of acknowledging harm, accepting responsibility for causing or contributing to that harm, and committing to making amends. On a body level, these processes take on a deeper dimension that allows us to engage in repair that feels real and authentic, rather than simply performative.

Strategies for Responding to an Embodied Microaggression You've Enacted

- Whenever possible, take time for a breath or two and to connect with a sense of spacious, grounded support in your body. Find in your body the quality of attention and presence that you want to bring into the interaction, whether that's openness, patience, compassion, respect, or curiosity. These qualities will shine through in your movements, expressions, breathing, and tone of voice, and they will show—rather than just say—your commitment to accountability.

- If you don't quite understand what you did that was upsetting or insulting to the other person, ask for clarification; just try not to make your request for clarification sound like a demand for proof. Once you're clear about your behavior and recognize how it was an unconscious expression of implicit bias, acknowledge the impact and connect it to the larger social justice issue. Focus on the impact rather than your intentions. Even if your behavior was not intentional, your intentions do not excuse your responsibility for your actions; nor do they erase the negative impact on the other person. When we accidentally bump into someone on a crowded street, we apologize and ask if the other person is all right. We don't belabor the fact that we didn't mean to do it.

- Offer what you can authentically give, whether that's an apology, making amends, or a commitment to changed behavior going forward.

- After the interaction is over, take a moment to return to an embodied experience of feeling spacious, grounded, and supported. Debrief with a trusted friend or colleague if that feels right.

Naming, disarming, and receiving feedback on the relational ruptures we experience every day isn't easy work. The memories of unsuccessful attempts to resolve or heal these paper cuts may haunt us for years afterward, coloring our willingness to reengage. How can we support ourselves and each other in the challenging task of shaping our interactions with one another so they are more aligned with the kind of world we want to live in?

Embodied Moral Courage

Never forget that justice is what love looks like in public.[9]

—CORNEL WEST

As the preceding section suggests, engaging in embodied activism in the context of our everyday relationships—with our dentist, our grocery clerk, our neighbors, and our family members—is not entirely without challenge or risk. It means disrupting old patterns of relating, asking hard questions, and presenting ourselves to the world in revealing and vulnerable ways. In other words, embodied activism requires courage.

Rushworth Kidder defines moral courage as the capacity to act in alignment with our values and principles in situations where they are being tested. He suggests that moral courage requires both a commitment to principles and a willingness to endure in the face of some risk to ourselves, such as our status, our reputation, our employment, or our membership in a valued social group. Kidder argues that moral courage can be learned and that there are several checkpoints in the process of developing moral courage.[10]

The first necessary skill in cultivating moral courage is the ability to assess a situation in terms of whether moral courage is even required. This idea might seem strange at first; after all, don't we want to be morally courageous all the time? However, there are situations in which it's important to question our motives and our choices before acting. Here are a few useful screening questions:

- Am I motivated by my desire to uphold my beliefs or merely to impose them on others? Is this situation calling me to do what's right, or is it possible that I'm unable to accept that others have different perspectives on the matter? When in the throes of outrage about a situation I feel is unjust, is it my values that are threatened, or mostly just my pride or self-interest? Am I responding from integrity rather than solely reacting from pain?

- Am I the best person to act? For example, am I taking over where I probably shouldn't and overriding someone else's agency? Conversely, does this situation call for me to move out of "bystander" mode and take action, even when I'm not centrally involved?

- Is now the best time? Sometimes the ideal moment to speak up or act out is in the freshness and immediacy of the here and now, when all the players are present and the impact of action will be felt by everyone. Other times, waiting until we've had a chance to reflect more deeply or marshal our resources is helpful. Consider whether this situation needs an audience or whether having a private interaction later would work better.

Once we know we need to act, it can then be helpful to tune into the moral principles at stake. Although we might initially experience the violation of our principles as a vague but compelling body sensation, being able to identify the core value that goes with those feelings can help us clarify the situation for ourselves and communicate it more clearly to others. According to research conducted at the Institute for Global Ethics, the five core values of honesty, responsibility, respect, fairness, and compassion are found in a range of social groups across many cultures. So, we might usefully ask ourselves, "Is there something about this situation that feels dishonest, irresponsible, disrespectful, unfair, or unkind?" Listening to how our body resonates with each question can help us home in on the nature of the relational rupture and affirm the need for moral courage.

Of course, situations requiring moral courage all carry some risk. Is it possible that speaking out or acting up is going to cause more harm than good? Who else will this affect? Will there be an impact beyond the immediate circle where the action is taken? It can also be helpful to assess our capacity to endure once action has been taken. Can we stick with this in the face of pushback, abandonment by others, or loss of resources? We don't necessarily want to be deterred by these risks, but we do want to be aware of them.

Emerging research in traumatology and social psychology suggests that learning to act on the courage of our convictions requires much more than just the capacity to assess situations, values, and risks. As relational beings who are wired for connection and whose survival depends in large part on how well we are treated by others, the marginalization and hostility directed at members of oppressed social groups can be experienced as an existential threat. In addition to real and threatened violence, nonviolent subjugation and implicit microaggressions can produce effects much like those of acute trauma. These effects include hypervigilance, constriction, and somatic reactivity in response to traumatic reminders.[11] When we add a demanding life or workload to a nervous system already compromised by the traumatic effects of oppression, there may be little bandwidth for navigating everyday power conflicts and injustices.

Consider the possibility that our own traumatic history of oppression may come into play in the present situation in ways that can feel disproportionately activating and charged. That's understandable. Fortunately, emerging trauma models suggest that body-centered strategies can be useful in recalibrating the somatic dysregulation so common in posttraumatic stress. Interventions that directly support the body in becoming more grounded, centered, and present can provide an important counterpoint to feelings of escalation and overwhelm. Getting resourced on a body level can help us clarify the best course of action and minimize the energetic cost of resisting injustice.

Connecting the research on moral courage to the findings in traumatology and social justice allows us to consider several additional factors in the cultivation of moral courage. First, members of oppressed social groups live in a world that is systemically unjust, where situations requiring moral courage can occur on an everyday basis. Dealing with them is exhausting, and tackling them all is impossible. Choosing our battles and being strategic is not a lack of moral courage. Also, expecting those with the least social power to take on the task—and risk—of righting all the wrongs enacted upon us is a further injustice. That said, even speaking up on behalf of others who have been wronged can be activating.

Given these complexities, the call for moral courage in the context of embodied activism requires a more intersectional analysis of the complex interrelationships between those involved in a situation and the systems and contexts in which these situations occur. We live in a complex, fluid social world in which the salient aspects of our multifaceted and evolving identities shift according to the unique dimensions of each new social context. Depending on the context, we can hold widely varying degrees of social power relative to others. Most of us have experienced being discriminated against based on our assigned membership in a particular social group, and most of us have treated others unjustly at some point in our lives. We bring these complex personal histories into our schools, communities, and workplaces, where they are further complicated by structural and group-based power dynamics. In other words, enacting moral courage is rarely a simple matter of defending "us" against "them."

Sociologist Robin D'Angelo coined the term "White fragility" to refer to White people's defensive reactions to accusations of racism. D'Angelo asserts that White people are so insulated from the pervasive stresses that people of color experience that many have a very limited capacity to endure the slightest exposure to their own White privilege.[12] Although a harsher term than *fragility* might be more fitting, the concept of fragility could be extended to other forms of unexamined and disowned privilege, and it lends itself to the notion that the antidote to fragility has something to do with becoming sturdier in some way. Certainly, it takes a kind of strength to hear criticism from members of social groups who hold less power, to accept responsibility for the harm one has caused (whether intentionally or not), and to make amends for that harm even when it comes at personal cost. I would argue that it also takes a commitment to the principles of fairness, compassion, honesty, responsibility, and respect—in short, moral courage.

If moral courage can be learned, as Rushworth Kidder suggests that it can, then it seems to me that the injunction to simply "feel the fear and do it anyway" seems inadequate for the complex demands and impulses that we navigate when we attempt to act on the courage of our convictions. Instead, perhaps we can learn to have more compassion for our fear. Rather than pushing past our bodily activation and dysregulation, perhaps we can learn to take steps to attend compassionately to them so our bodies can help us do the right thing. And of course, responding to injustice with integrity does not mean being nice or swallowing our anger. It means anchoring our feelings in our principles and in an intercorporeal ethos.

BODY STORY
The Role of the Body in Moral Courage

A couple of years ago, Ayesha (her name is a pseudonym, and her story is used with permission) was at a professional training event in her field. Following a moderated panel presentation in a large ballroom, the Q and A session evolved into a sustained discussion among the panelists about one panelist's experience in working with body dysmorphia among disabled people in a clinical treatment group. As the conversation became increasingly clinical and abstract, a member of the audience came up to the microphone and, with restrained but visible emotion, noted that the panelists seemed to be talking about folks with disabilities as if they were a fascinating but exotic clinical specimen. The audience member pointed out that disabled people were not something to be examined as if they were somehow "over there" in a special clinical population, but were in fact "right here," in the room. The moderator looked at the audience member, thanked them for their comment, and briskly moved on to a completely different topic.

Have you ever been in a room when it quietly but rapidly catches fire? That's what happened here. Ayesha turned and looked at her colleagues sitting on either side of her and raised her eyebrow. One of her colleagues whispered under their breath, "Did that just happen?" and Ayesha replied, "Apparently, it just did." Here and there around the room, delegates were turning to one another, shifting in their seats, and muttering among themselves. Clearly, several members of the audience were having a hard time believing that the moderator could have so thoroughly invalidated and dismissed a thoughtful request that the panel speak to the "othering" that had been occurring.

Immediately, Ayesha realized that she needed to get up, walk across the room to the microphone, and ask the moderator if they could please go back to the point that had just been made by the previous questioner. As soon as that impulse arose in her body—to get up, to move, and to speak—a nearly simultaneous internal response also occurred. Ayesha's heart began racing, her face went hot, her throat tightened, and her stomach dropped. She began having trouble taking a full breath. She said she felt "as though my engine was revving at incredible speed while my foot was stamped firmly on the brakes."

As Ayesha struggled with her bodily experience, her mind was also doing interesting things. She asked herself if perhaps she was overreacting and wondered if her boss (who was in the room) would think she was a troublemaker if she spoke up. As Ayesha debated with herself, the conversation moved on. Then, just as she was telling herself that it was too late and the moment had passed to say anything, someone else went up to the mic and did what Ayesha felt too afraid to do: they spoke up, respectfully, calmly, and thoughtfully. According to Ayesha, their redirection back to the microaggression was a transformative moment for the audience, moderator, and panelists alike, and a small but important turning point for her field. Unpacking this experience has led Ayesha to become more curious about the role the body plays in the enactment of courage, particularly when justice is on the line.

EMBODIED PRAXIS
Finding Your Feet, Spine, Heart, and Voice

Imagine a situation in which something has occurred that feels unfair or unjust to you—nothing too big or too raw, but unjust all the same. Now imagine that you are speaking out against that injustice, perhaps saying "I'm not okay with what just happened" or words to that effect. As you imagine speaking the words, notice how your body responds.

Now, take a moment to take a breath, noticing the inhale and exhale. Bring your awareness to your feet, feeling them connected solidly to the ground. Next, feel inside to find your spine, allowing it to find its length. Anchor your spine in your hips, and let your shoulders rest on your rib cage. Then bring your awareness to your heart. And finally bring awareness to your throat, finding your voice. Now, imagine again that you are speaking out, saying "I'm not okay with what just happened." And notice any difference in how that feels this time.

Although the cultivation of embodied moral courage is a lifelong pursuit, each new interaction is an opportunity to strengthen the muscles that help us stand upright under duress, without hardening those same muscles into a kind of body armor that prevents us from feeling the humanity of others. The following interview offers a glimpse into the life's work of community organizer Dr. Sam Grant and how he has navigated the relational challenges of organizing for social and environmental justice, in and through his body.[13]

Cultivating Somatic Bandwidth through Mutual Engagement: An Interview with Sam Grant

Rae: Please say a little bit about how you understand the ways in which the social body comes into play in your work. This notion of the social body can get so theoretical. I'm really interested in hearing how you make it real and relational.

Sam: I have been an organizer and facilitator for over three decades, working with grassroots and intersectional formations all over the United States, Africa, the Caribbean, South America, and Canada. And for me, the work has always been about how do we adjust to and with each other? How do we mutually discern how the world is working through us and how stuck patterns in the world around us are inhibiting what we're hoping to realize in our lives on a day-to-day basis? It's about mutuality and mutual wellness. All my work since I began organizing is about mutual liberation.

Yet when a lot of people talk about the body, they want to focus on my individual body. Western civilization is stuck on "me"—what do I want, decontextualized from the consequential impacts of being ego-centered and not eco-centered—and it embodies what I consider to be pathological narcissism as normalized in terms of what it looks like to live the good life. It is competitive individualism at mass scale. As a cultural worker, I strive to do what Amílcar Cabral calls us to do in the African diaspora, which is to "return to our source" and act as a resource for cultural and mutual liberation from there, which is the intercultural work.

This does not make sense to a lot of people who feel it is impossible to access cultural roots that underlie colonial and imperial impositions. The intercultural work does not make sense to a lot of people who are sick and tired of being asked to join coalition efforts when their own needs are dismissed or minimized in such environments. I have spent a lifetime working out how to respond to the challenges. I see all this work as the work of *deep democracy:* cocreating conditions in the world that foster the flourishing of all of life.

Thinking about the African cosmological concept of *ubuntu*—"I am because we are"—I begin from *we,* and then I take responsibility for my contribution to *us.* I'm always weaving and braiding this interplay of sensibilities we have in terms of attitude, in terms of behavior, in terms of process, that we bring alive through our work in the world. Twenty-plus years ago I was very impacted by the work of Stephen Biko, who was one of the leaders of the black consciousness movement in South Africa. He had this quote that he used that I have been recycling ever since, which is: "The greatest weapon in the hands of the oppressor is the mind of the oppressed." My amendment to what he said is, "It's actually the body." When my body is no longer tuned in to what it wants to create for itself, in terms of its relationship from inner habitat to relational habitat to world habitat, then it's a metaphor for what Frantz Fanon said in his work *Black Skin, White Masks:* to be a person who's colonized is to live in the zone of nonbeing.

The world-ecological history of colonialism and imperialism has removed most of us from mutually determining capacities and conditions and imposed the leviathan of global corporate capitalism grounded in colonialism, imperialism, heteropatriarchy, genocide, and anti-Black violence. The corporeal body of the corporation matters far more than that of human bodies and cultures, water bodies, climate systems, and so on.

You're living in a social structure that refuses your existence and certainly refuses your value. As a person who in my own identity braids a Black and Indigenous perspective on who I am and what I'm trying to be a resource for on the planet, that means that I need to end genocide and I need to end anti-Black violence. And because I'm in the world with people with complex identities, I have to find a way to share that journey, to be thoroughly relational, and deeply democratic, in all my relations on this journey. For me to share that journey, part of my somatic practice as an individual is to think of myself metaphorically as a tuning fork. As I think about my dialogue with you, I'm thinking about how you and I tune into a new mutual channel that's as open as possible. I notice that on days like today, when I did not take time and space to ground and invite the most mutual conversation possible, that is imposing a challenge to what emerges through me for us today. And that requires a practice of vulnerability and a nourishing of the space of covulnerability. We can adapt and improvise but also slow things down as we need to, to make sure there's a mutual process of adjustment that's iterative and coevolving through time.

In 2001 I was doing a workshop on internalized oppression for a social justice organization. And Zea (who is now my wife) was there at the workshop. She came up to me at the end of it and she gave me a very important critique. She said, "You are talking to people about internalized oppression. It's never going to work. Oppression is in the body, and you have to help people deal with it from an embodied vantage point." And I said, "Tell me more." And that was the start of our relationship.

Rae: You were using that tuning fork already, right? Instead of steeling yourself and refusing her critique, you just went, "Oh, how do I resonate with that?"

Sam: Yeah. So, I took that in, and then she told me about her work with a mentor of hers who had studied process work and was really into this notion of deep democracy. I listened to her talk about deep democracy from the way they talked about it in that particular container. And I said, "I have always resonated with the notion of deep democracy, but I have a different orientation to it than that one." Mine is, dialectically, an acolonial (sourcing from precolonial knowledges) and decolonial (sourcing from capacities to disrupt what harms wellness in relation at all scales) orientation to deep democracy because from my vantage point, it's the original process by which human beings related with each other and with nature. It's nondivisive. Nonexcludable. Humble. Open. Relational. In fact, even to go further, sacred. All of life is sacred. Our bodies are sacred. Our relationships are sacred. Our insights and our friction points—they're all sacred.

How do we bring loving energy to all of that? So that instead of being a fist to each other, we can soften, and we can unwind in relationship both within ourselves and then in the relationship. So, when I'm working in a group setting, I'm paying attention to people's embodied signals. What am I presencing to them, what are they showing me, how are we interpreting the signals we pick up from each other verbally and nonverbally? Working with those signals that I receive, I do my best to bring resonant awareness to it, which means not to impose an answer or a judgment, but to lean in with a question.

For example, if I am talking to someone, as I did today about a strategy to end homelessness, I can say: "Can you tell me more about what you mean when you talk about how you are experiencing the intersectionality of mental health challenges and structural racism in the task of trying to end homelessness? Tell me more about your narrative and where you feel stuck." Then the person is invited to vulnerably tell a story. They are more likely open to shift their position from telling an analytical narrative to telling an embodied narrative. People in the group then receive them in a different place. People come down to this deeper level, and they're in storytelling mode as well. It's no longer abstract. I suggest it is not that difficult to notice whether you are co-resonating with people you are in relation with. We just need to pay attention to it and take co-responsibility for it.

Rae: What I hear you saying is that when you invite someone into their own narrative—"tell me what that was like, tell me how that felt, tell me what was going on for you and what's going on for you in your body"—then all of a sudden, what's going on in the room is so much more relatable. Because our bodies are tuning forks and it makes a real difference when someone will let their body resonate with their own experience, not just to discharge it, but to engage others in it.

Sam: Exactly. We live in stories and through the stories we tell. In a world where many of us get conditioned to be rational and stay trapped in head space, we set ourselves up for not being able to hear each other. We create cultures where deep listening becomes less possible, rather than more. Deep democracy invites us to channel stories from our lived experience and from that place within us that is open to being a resource for mutuality. How we show up in a space is always having an impact on whoever is in that space with us. For us to be intentional, not here [points to head] but here [points to heart], about the vibration we want to transmit has a profound impact on what's possible. I've made this mistake as an "activist" in the pejorative construct of being an activist—that you're muscular and you're fighting the system—and I've realized (slower than I would like) just how destructive it is to come with that *break it down and burn it all* kind of energy. It felt good sometimes, and necessary even when it didn't, until people came into my life with a wiser energy and helped me heal beyond fight-flight-freeze-fawn, and zero sum. For all life to matter, we have to bring equitable care to all of life.

I'm learning slowly to bring more loving energy consistently, and I'm learning somatic processes of reregulating and coregulating myself. Saying to myself, "Wait a minute, I could react, or I could respond." And to respond instead. My language around responding is that it's mutually generative. It's creating conditions in which I can be where I am in terms of having a perspective, but I need to acknowledge that my perspective is just that—it's my perspective. You have your perspective. Let's continue to unfold together in this middle space and find a connecting point that then allows us to have some confidence that what's going on in this interaction is not intractable, it's *in process*. Part of the work is recognizing that my perspective comes from somewhere, and so does yours. By sourcing from lived experience and bringing consciousness about the extent to which there is dissonance or resonance between what we say, do, feel, dream, share, we cocreate capacities for mutual liberation.

Part of the trap of the West is the fast pace at which we live. We have been disrupted from slow time and slow process with ourselves and each other, and we have got to take it back. And to recognize that things are in process and to bring the wisdom of patience, but also the wisdom of nudging. So, there's always this nudging in the space of our edges, but it's paying attention to what happens in terms of what's the appropriate nudge for Sam to give in this particular context.

And I need to learn. And with some people I do that really well, and in some places I fail miserably because I can't get out of my own way.

Rae: Or there are times when the nudge feels like a push, even though you didn't mean it as a push.

Sam: Right. In my Black body, anything I say or do in relation to Whiteness that is perceived as a threat to its comfort, privilege, and power is perceived as a push, not a loving nudge. Within communal spaces that I sense are affinity spaces, we can surprisingly fall dangerously out of alignment by overassuming our level of coherence.

Let's examine the developmental sequence of yield-push-reach-grasp-pull in this context. If we foster healthy co-resonance in relation, we can yield together and push together, and that sets up what we can sustainably pull through together. When what we are sensing in our yield—observing, bringing awareness to signals in the field—is out of alignment, what we push for will be too. That is not bad if we can coadjust. Are we willing and able to coadjust? What role do power dynamics and internalized oppression play in our willingness and capacity to coadjust?

Rae: I'm hearing how important it is for you to slow things down, but also noticing a quality of spaciousness and ongoingness that I think lots of people in the moment—particularly the hot moments—somehow forget, which is that even if they never speak to a certain invididual again, they're very likely going to be speaking with someone from a similar location, position, or perspective again.

Sam: Guaranteed. So how do I want to deal with this? How do I engage with this idea that these aren't intractable problems, they're issues and perspectives in tension, given underlying divided realities of eco-apartheid in the world? We have been structurally divided by religion, by geography, by ideology, by access lines to power and privilege, by access to or no access to ecological space on a self-determined basis, and the list goes on. If you have privilege and power and you are *over there* [points away], free to roam in spaces I cannot access because I lack the access card of whatever form, and you only enter spaces I am in as a voyeur or extractor, how can we ever cocreate conditions for mutuality? We cannot until we commit to a mutual determination of what deep mutuality requires.

Whether it's with you or with someone else, this is the world we live in—a world of structurally violent divisiveness, which we only see when it *hits* us. I am calling up that quote: first they came for the Indigenous people, and no one was there in solidarity. Then they came for the peasants, and no one had their back. Then they came for the workers, and there were few people left who might give a damn. Then they came for you, and, of course, you were then doomed. That's not the quote, but it is an articulation of the violent, destructive energy of the divisiveness in our world.

There's a school of philosophy in Nigeria called the Calabar School. Several scholars in that school are working on different orientations of this notion of complementarity. One of these scholars says that all perspectives are a missing link in our shared reality. And so, if I greet you from a place of mutual curiosity—"Tell me more about that perspective. This is new to me."—I'm going to invite it in as a teacher. I'll be a humble student of this alternative perspective on the planet.

Learning that orientation from Africana philosophy has been a very important tool for me to metabolize and bring into my day-to-day practice when I'm working in a group context. For example, I could be working with a group at the grassroots level who has never had space with city officials where they feel like they were talking to each other as real peers. When I finally get those two groups to be in a common space where the structural reality of power inequality falls away temporarily to make space for hearing each other, then part of my objective is to help them carry the energy from this momentary equality back into day-to-day relationships on an ongoing basis. It's not easy, because there are defaults that run through us in terms of power dynamics on the planet. People with significant power can discredit or destroy social formations that are requesting healthier relationship. For much of human history, that request for healthier relationship has been ignored or violated.

My work as a social somatic practitioner is to help people in social spaces bring our best selves forward, according to where we're aligned on something we want to cocreate in the world. Supporting each other where we each have different kinds of gaps in our capacity to stay in comanifestation mode. There's a level of vulnerability here that is mapped onto power dynamics. If my power is not disrupted, I am not all that likely to disrupt myself. Mutual power is an interrelational, intercommunal process that is always flowing.

So, for me, the work of deep democracy is sourcing from this notion of mutuality. How do we foster common wellness for you and me and for everybody in our shared ecosystem? Part of deep democracy work is coming back to my source of what do I really want to create here? Not from here [pointing to head], but from here [pointing to heart]. What do I really want to create, going through a whole cycle of self-reflection and then dialogic reflection? What are the things that are at my edge and at your edge, and how do we all learn from each other's edges so that we work through those edges instead of retreating from those edges? Those with power and privilege tend to want to retreat to comfort. They're not willing to be unsettled for more than a few seconds.

Rae: They don't yet have muscles for it.

Sam: Right. So how do we grow each other's muscles—capacities plus commitments—for staying in unsettled terrain? How do we induce and sustain a tolerable level of somatic disequilibrium, to use the term from your book *Embodied Social Justice?*

Rae: And I'm guessing that you don't want folks to learn to tolerate more discomfort. We don't want anyone to be gritting their teeth and bracing and muscling through a difficult moment in a relationship or in an interaction. Because so many of us have to do that all the bloody time. We don't want to use the muscle of tolerating pain when that muscle is already overdeveloped. So, I get curious about how this muscle of somatic disequilibrium is different. I have the feeling that in your work with others, you've noticed people who are holding so much privilege that they don't have much muscle for this work at all, and people who have been so disenfranchised that the muscles for gritting their teeth or for lashing out are their go-to muscles. For you, what does it feel like in those moments when people in an engagement are reaching toward or able to sustain a bodily sensation of disequilibrium? And how do you support that? I know that's a huge question.

Sam: It's an important question. One of the things that I have been doing since I was very young in this work is paying attention to the reality that if we're going to work together, we need to establish some simple rules and protocols in the container of our work so we stay in that container in a way that's mutually functional. We have to have a strategy for when things get too hot. If somebody needs to exit and then return, how are they supported if they need to exit and return? And then how do we not marginalize the fact that somebody needed to exit, but actually make that a learning agenda for everybody?

When people ask me how I am doing, I will often respond, "Ridiculous!" Most people do not know how to interpret that and assume it's a bad thing or that I am a joker bringing light energy to the question and being open to being real rather than superficial. People usually respond with alarm, or with laughter, jarring surprise, or delight. What do I mean by *ridiculous?* I think it's ridiculous and unnecessary to live in a world organized around division, fear, and violence. So, as a person standing for something different, I feel the dissonance between my values and how the world works, and the resonance among people who do their best to bring that other possible world alive in the present moment.

So, somatic disequilibrium is present in edge spaces. People with power may wield it to make the disequilibrium experience continue on your side of the tension, but not allow it to continue on their side. They may bring "White tears" to disrupt with White fragility praxis or bring up the mythical power of the White superhero image they may hold of themselves in a moment, and in either of these ways block mutuality. A person on the downside of power might express Black fatigue or some form of self-righteous, rebellious, or revolutionary militancy. We cause trouble for ourselves and each other when we refuse to "stay with the trouble."

All of the world has been organized somatically to follow a particular power path, in which most of us have very little power, or face the consequences. To invite people to remain in spaces of somatic disequilibrium with ourselves and with other and to be generative and cogenerative within the context of this experiential disequilibrium is the work of the twenty-first century.

We can continue to wreck ecological systems and allow reckless human systems to run over all of life and each other, or we can honor the mantra of the great poet, now ancestor, Kirk Washington Jr. and ask ourselves along with him, "we already know how to be divided, what I really want to know is how we can come together?" Like Audre Lorde told us so clearly, we cannot build a mutual house with the master's tools based on dividing us; we have to learn how to be in somatic disequilibrium long enough to see our way clearly to a mutually satisfactory social somatic equilibrium. It is for this reason that Zea Leguizamon, Jennifer Kleskie, and I, the core principals of Embody Deep Democracy, have been exploring and experimenting with what we and others call the emerging space/field/praxis of social somatics. To grow a mutual world ecology, we have to get past zero sum. In too many cases, people with greater structural power disrupt what is emerging in the perennial dialogues seeking mutuality because they have the power to do so.

For example, there's a negative stereotype about certain women of color being hotheaded—too emotional and too heavy-handed with what they bring into a space. They're labeled for making White women and White men feel unsafe. I had a situation in an earlier work environment where I had several organizational members come to me and demand that I fire somebody because of this person's unsettling behavior. And I said to them, "I hear you, but I'm not going to do that." Part of tolerating somatic disequilibrium is being grounded in the values that you hold as a practitioner and being transparent about those values. So, what I said to them is, "I hear you, but I don't have a sense that you are encompassing the other perspective. All of you share a narrative about this person, and I don't think it's that simple. I think there's something in this person's process and practice and message that would be useful for you to attend to. Are you open to that at all?" And they were not open to attending to that at all. They were adamant that this staff member needed to go. And so I said, "If you need to terminate somebody, please go to the board and have them fire me, because I'm not going to do it. I'm going to facilitate a process that tries to bring us together. But I'm not going to throw somebody under the bus, because I operate from a principle of nonexclusion." My stance and process did not work out well for any of us in this instance.

Please understand that I'm not Pollyannish about this. Things don't always work out with everyone all the time. But I feel like there's an appropriate process of giving things a try, and everybody needs to take responsibility for that. And in this case, people weren't willing to budge. Unfortunately, in this situation that person felt the resistance to honoring anything that they were bringing and decided to resign. That was a loss for us, because that person was bringing a very critical kind of work into that social arena. The organization now doesn't get the benefit of that.

For me as a practitioner, I have to go back to that moment and think about what I might have done differently in that space to facilitate an actual softening in the rigid stance that was being taken. I was really disappointed in my staff at that moment. And my disappointment reinforced the need for me to sit at their feet individually and make the request for a little bit of openness. If I had switched it from a group attack to a one-to-one dialogue to see where people are, then I could bring the group back together to see whether there's any mutual softness or openness to a different adaptation. And I didn't do that process. I noticed a defensive embodied stance I took up, which was a counterproductive stance. And rather than doing the inner work to let it go, I reinforced it. I justified it.

Rae: You defended the person who was being attacked, but it was still a defense.

Sam: Yup. Not only did I defend the person who was being attacked, I defended my justification and made the folks who brought in the concern the problem instead. I didn't mean to do that, but that's how it worked out. In a divisive situation, I added divisive energy—the self-righteous energy mentioned above. This notion of nonexcludability matters to me. When people exit, they take a perspective with them that is living in the world. The people remaining in space need that perspective in order to attend, with wisdom, to dynamics in the whole. Easier said than done.

Rae: Would you speak to the role of compassion in supporting someone in softening?

Sam: It goes back to what we talked about at the beginning. I'd rather use the word *empathy*. It's the vibrational effect. With compassion, you are still "the other." With empathy, we are joined in feeling something. Empathy emerges when you get people to talk beneath the story or to speak from their lived experience, rather than the rationalization of it in their head, and we generate story energy together that we both feel.

With really good questions, people will tend to unfold. It's in the unfolding that we encounter this space of covulnerability, where things can emerge so you can recognize different options. Part of the work is just to meet people with compassion. Acknowledge that they're heard. Because until people feel heard, they are a block, they're a stone; they're not water. You want people to name their stone. Then you want people to be the water that washes over the stone. So you bring them to a place of being able to practice. The work of social somatics is always learning to be a resource, a catalyst for a mutual opening and then to see what happens there. So yes, compassion and empathy as practices of loving regard for all people and all of life sit at the root of all of this work.

Rae: I'm hearing that although there might be moves you could make or strategies you could enlist, the base of it is finding that quality in your own body that you would like to invite the other person into. If I'm experiencing someone else as defensive or argumentative or unreasonable or checked out, I need to find the counterpoint in my own body and be it.

Sam: And I will only know how to be it if I've done enough listening. Part of my process is to pay attention to who's going to be in a space and to have an informal interview with them first. I let them know that we're about to have this container that we're both going to be in. I want to know what's exciting for you about being in that container. And I want to know what's disturbing for you about being in that container. Do you have any bottom-line objectives you want to see happen in that container? And do you have any bottom-line things that you want to not be included in that container?

When they can tell me what those bottom lines are for them, I can then go in and honor and work my own tuning fork. I can ask myself what's going to happen if this particular pattern emerges in the group. If this person has told me they can't tolerate something, what can I do in my own body vibrationally? That sets up a condition where maybe that person who is going to run from the container, I'm going to be able to notice that the thing that they can't accept is emerging, and I can pay attention to them. I can give them loving regard from where they're sitting in the room. I've got you here. Stay with me. And just that simple nonverbal cue can sometimes help people stay. Just reminding people to breathe, but I have to be a resource for that. I get tuned in to what people are bringing, and then I can amplify the kind of responsive repertoire that I need both for that person and for the group as a whole. To stay in the space, or as Donna Haraway talks about it, stay with the trouble. Stay with the trouble. Trouble is here, but it's not a bad thing. It's good medicine.

I do my own limited version of this when I am working with diverse groups coming with all different kinds of baggage and possibilities. When I have the time and space to do so, I dialogue with people individually before they enter the space and do a little creative work with them to prepare them to enter from their higher, more open vibration, and discern what they need from me and the group to stay open. When possible, I also seek to make arrangements for a safe exit and return if things get too hot for them.

We need to consider how we cocreate social conditions for our full selves to be present and remain in a stance of openness, cocuriousity, covulnerability. Then we need to commit to carry back what we experienced (without violating confidentiality) and what we learned to influence people in our distinct influence networks toward increasing mutuality.

Rae: I'm noticing this real attention that you pay to the process of informed consent.

Sam: It's not just, "We're on, and let's see what happens." It's, "Let's have a conversation before we come into this conversation." And let's be partners in the mutual unfolding of what happens in space and pay attention to what is allowed in terms of what we are capable of working on together and what throws us into a level of somatic disequilibrium that is too much in that space and that moment.

Rae: Let's talk a bit about working with somatic bandwidth. I'm hearing you say that if you don't know how much folks can tolerate, then you don't know when the situation is going to exceed their capacity. So, they're understandably going to revert to the same patterns and the same interactional style that got everyone stuck in the first place. I'm really hearing this important first step of ensuring that people are participating voluntarily with an understanding of what they're getting into. But also, when the trouble arrives, when the dynamic emerges that they're having a hard time being with by themselves, they don't have to be with it by themselves anymore because you can be there with them.

Sam: Exactly. It's accompanying people on the journey toward mutual liberation. In that space as a practitioner, I am an accomplice to the person or institution that has made a mistake. And I'm an accomplice to the person or institution who is naming what the mistake was. And I'm fostering a condition in which the person or institution will continue to name the mistake but also articulate what it would look like if this wasn't the continuing pattern. I seek the normalization of people tracking with each other, inclusive of right and wrong, but not stuck in either/or thinking (zero-sum behavior). Moving toward mutuality requires an imagination of what is possible beyond being stuck, and a trust in our mutual capacities to sustainably move in that direction.

Then my question to the person or institution is, "Can you adapt? Can you braid the perspectives you exclude into your own perspective to become a resource for an inclusive perspective? Are you willing to adapt? What does it look like for you to adapt? How long will it take you for to adapt? When will you know if you've adapted appropriately? How do you adjust your pace so that it's a relational pace? What might be going on in you and/or the institution that prevents openness here?"

Rae: Sometimes people with power and good intentions believe that they can unilaterally set a goal and it will be good for everyone. But that's not the goal of mutuality.

Sam: That's right. And mutuality does not mean universality. We have differences that do not disappear and ought to be honored. Protecting the remaining Indigenous languages in the world that sustain life in the last remaining habitats with significant biological diversity means honoring diverse modes of existence and the relational possibilities and tensions among them. bell hooks talked about it as something she called polyphonic vocality. Cheikh Anta Diop talked about the need to develop a polyversal scientific capacity that honors diverse ways of knowing and brings them into relation. Gregory Cajete speaks to this as well in his articulation of Native science. And I love the way Robin Wall Kimmerer gets at it in *Braiding Sweetgrass.* The concept of braiding is at the core of nourishing conditions of mutuality for me.

And the only way the goal can be mutuality is if there's an ongoing, always opening, always evolving, deeply democratic dialogue, where you're directly talking to people who've been excluded from the conversation, excluded from the design. Open design processes are critical in cocreating a world that fosters mutual thriving. We haven't had that world for the last five thousand years. But we're at a point of crystallization where enough people realize that the way we've allowed things to run doesn't serve the earth. Doesn't serve human beings. Bringing awareness is one step, but awareness isn't enough. Because our patterns are sticky. And the relationships that reinforce those patterns that we hold in our bodies are also sticky. So part of the work is asking people to pay more attention to the values that they really wish to live by and inviting them into this discourse about ways that, through our relationships, we can unfold in a way that is mutually supportive of common well-being.

Finally, that power thing. People with structural and cultural power and unearned or stolen privileges are reluctant to yield power, even when they throw rhetoric around about equity, justice, and mutuality. Two things Martin Luther King Jr. said stay with me as markers for how real and ready folks are for mutual liberation. In his letter from the Birmingham jail, he offered a critique of White liberals as "fair weather"—only with you when it is convenient for them. In 1967, in his "Beyond Vietnam" speech—significantly contributed to by the powerhouse historian, now ancestor, Vincent Harding—he defined three evils that keep us from coming together: organized impoverishment, organized global-scale militarism (a weapon of ecological imperialism), and globalized racism (dividing us from each other based on physical differences). He asked us back then, where do we go from here, chaos or community? It is high time to answer affirmatively that we are ready for and committed to mutual liberation.

Embodying Mutuality

In the preceding interview, Sam Grant talks about the need to cultivate a relational mutuality as a viable alternative to continually reenacting oppressive power dynamics in our interactions with others. Earlier in the book, Niki Koumoutsos, Kaleb Sinclair, and Sean Ambrose discuss the importance of deep connection to others. How might we begin to embody these new ways of being with one another? Drawing from the material in this chapter, here are four overarching strategies that focus specifically on how we can bring our bodies into our practice of mutual liberation.

1. **Cultivate somatic bandwidth**. This involves becoming more comfortable with feeling, witnessing, and expressing a wide range of embodied emotions and sensations. Where our bodies are in pain due to the oppressive conditions we live in, creating more spaciousness around that pain helps us to remember that there's not anything inherently wrong with us; rather, the pain is about what's happened to us. Cultivating our somatic bandwidth also means exploring and reenlivening those places in our body where we experience numbness, emptiness, or lack of feeling. Expanding our somatic bandwidth offers us more choices in our body about how we respond to situations—internal and external—and while those choices can include settling and calming responses, somatic bandwidth isn't about downregulating or deactivating in the face of injustice. Rather, a broad, flexible bandwidth supports us in staying more connected to our full embodied experience (without being hijacked by it) when working to address and transform injustice. It also offers more capacity to be with somatic disequilibrium when it arises by learning to be more comfortable in the temporary discomfort that comes from engaging in new ways.

2. **Practice kinesthetic empathy**. When hearing someone describe their experience or their understanding of an event, kinesthetic empathy asks us to imagine what it might feel like in our body to experience what they've gone through. It encourages us to be curious and attentive, using

our own capacity for embodied presence and engaged responsiveness to listen and empathize without imposing our own experience or taking over. Kinesthetic empathy allows us to take in the lived, embodied experience of others and to be moved by it without losing ourselves in it. At the same time, even when our capacity for kinesthetic empathy is well developed, it's important not to assume that we know everything we need to know about what it feels like to live in their skin. Rather, it's about learning to love their bodies as we've learned to love our own. Also, having kinesthetic empathy does not mean being "nice," avoiding conflict, or failing to set boundaries. Rather, it means that when we bring sharpness, fierceness, and strength to our interactions with each other, we do more than just consider the possible impact of these qualities on others; we are prepared to feel *in our bodies* the ripple effect of our actions in the relationship and in the world.

3. **Listen with our bodies.** Our bodies are an incredible source of information when we learn to listen to their inner sensations, intuitions, and impulses. But we can listen to other bodies, too, not just our own. For example, we can accommodate for our privilege when interacting with those with less power by listening to them more attentively with our body, and by noticing when others appear physically uncomfortable, distant, or anxious, or when they show visible signs of being overly agreeable. While we might not always read those body signals correctly, we can always ask, "Are you okay?" and then really listen to the answer. In those situations where we hold less power, we can tune into the bodily signals that let us know how safe we feel and whether we're ready to engage or need to withdraw.

4. **Engage our bodies.** When we choose to act, it's important to appreciate the potency of our bodily gestures when "standing up" for our principles or "reaching out" to others. We don't always need a lot of words to get our message across. Our bodies can speak louder than words.

In the following poem, Danusha Laméris reflects on the everydayness of these mutual interactions and how our hopes and yearnings for a more just world can be realized in the small moments of connection that make up our lives. Although our response to injustice may show up as fierceness as often as it shows up as kindness, Laméris beautifully portrays the degree to which intercorporeality—our bodily embeddedness in one another—means attending to all the ways in which we can choose to open (or close) one another's hearts.

Small Kindnesses[14]

I've been thinking about the way, when you walk
down a crowded aisle, people pull in their legs
to let you by. Or how strangers still say "bless you"
when someone sneezes, a leftover
from the Bubonic plague. "Don't die," we are saying.
And sometimes, when you spill lemons
from your grocery bag, someone else will help you
pick them up. Mostly, we don't want to harm each other.
We want to be handed our cup of coffee hot,
and to say thank you to the person handing it. To smile
at them and for them to smile back. For the waitress
to call us honey when she sets down the bowl of clam chowder,
and for the driver in the red pickup truck to let us pass.
We have so little of each other, now. So far
from tribe and fire. Only these brief moments of exchange.
What if they are the true dwelling of the holy, these
fleeting temples we make together when we say, "Here,
have my seat," "Go ahead—you first," "I like your hat."

—DANUSHA LAMÉRIS

Learning from Our Intercorporeal Engagements

Embodied activism is a practice, not a destination. It's an incremental, developmental process. With each engagement, big or small, we have an opportunity to shift the small patterns that help create the larger structures in our world. And with each shift, we learn more about how our bodies shape our engagements with others. Here are some questions that can help provide a springboard for reflection as we process what's happened and how we might orient ourselves for the next interaction.

- How did I feel in my body going into this interaction? What sensations, qualities, or movement impulses were occurring before this interaction occurred?

- What power dynamics were present in the interaction? How did I feel them on a body level?
- What nonverbal communication occurred during the interaction that feels important or meaningful?
- What actions did I take on a body level? How did they shape the engagement?
- How do I feel in my body now that the interaction is over?
- How might this interaction inform my next engagement with this person or group of people? Somatically, is there anything I would like to do differently?

Taking the time to reflect on our embodied engagements with others can offer two important benefits. First, it provides an opportunity to get some closure on interactions that may not have gone particularly well or that have left us with some questions or unsettled feelings. Second, the process of somatically sifting through these experiences helps us learn from them in ways that are not just cognitive but allow what we've learned to live in our bodies, shaping them in ways that are more attuned to our values and commitments.

Intercorporeality and the More-Than-Human World

Environmental justice activists are increasingly linking the health of the planet to the well-being of our own bodies, not just in terms of the health impacts of pollution, climate change, and industrialized food production, but also the long-term consequences of being disconnected from our primal natures. Many of these activists understand a focus on embodiment as central to their tasks of making visible the issues of environmental justice in the lives of marginalized communities and of interrogating the toxicity of everyday landscapes. Of course, it's not just about how an ailing natural world affects the human species. In intercorporeal terms, many of us are living in the context of an abusive relationship with the natural world—one in which we are the perpetrator. The next section of this chapter offers some practical strategies that the reader can engage to shift from viewing the natural world as an increasingly fragile resource for human consumption to experiencing the earth body and the human body as inextricably interwoven aspects of each other.

earth mother inside/inside mother earth

i am reclaiming my body land
cells like drops of rain on open fields
sinking in and drinking deeply of the knowledge in my bones
i am putting my hands on the planet
i am lying full length face down into the earth
and we are revolving in space together
through me and throughout me
the mother reconnects us
this arm . . . that hill . . . this ankle
the wide curve of water and stone that is the belly of the sea
when i roll over to face the sky
the depth of it sends me reeling
i catch my breath
inhaling sky . . . exhaling me
the mother weaves the world and me together
in the light of day, she illuminates me
in the dark of night, she links constellations within my skin
we both have stars in our eyes as
she tells me with her body
and i tell her with mine
if this is the universe
we must be home

As the preceding poem suggests, it's possible to cultivate a relationship with the natural world that is grounded in mutuality. In the same way that we engage our bodies to support an intercorporeal ethos with other humans, similar strategies can help us strengthen our sense of deep mutual belonging with the plants, animals, rivers, clouds, and mountains whose fates—for better or worse—we share.

Even those of us who live in urban environments have countless everyday engagements with the natural world: we shovel the snow from our sidewalks, boil water for tea, bask in a puddle of sunlight pouring in from a window. We take a deep breath of early morning air, watch squirrels race nimbly across telephone wires, and slice carrots for dinner. Although some of us have the privilege of "retreat"-ing to spend time in the wilderness—and while these immersions in nature can be a balm for tired, industrialized souls—it's not necessary to leave our everyday lives in order to embrace our connections with the living, sentient beings that surround us.

> *Movement is the great law of life. Everything moves. The heavens move, the earth turns, the great tides mount the beaches of the world. The clouds march slowly across the sky, driven by a wind that stirs the trees into a dance of branches. Water, rising in the mountain springs, runs down the slopes to join the current of the river. Fire, begun in the brush, leaps roaring over the ground. And the Earth, so slow, so always there, grumbles and groans and shifts in the sleep of the centuries.*
>
> —*MARY WHITEHOUSE* [15]

EMBODIED PRAXIS
Engaging the More-Than-Human Others

Choose an element of the more-than-human world that you engage with in your everyday life and whose presence in your life calls to you, or where your relative disconnection from that element troubles you. It can be as simple and humble as the water you drink, as complex as the relationship you have with a pet, or as mysterious as the network of mushrooms that emerge in your backyard after a summer rain.

Notice all the sensory qualities and dimensions of this element of the world—its shape, color, sound, and texture. Notice how it moves, or what moves it. Pay attention to how your body responds as you engage with its body.[16] Then allow yourself to consider how you would feel in your body if this more-than-human other was not in your life, or if its body were weakened, sullied, compromised, or injured (and perhaps this is already the case). Reflect on the network of relationships and connections this element has with other aspects of the natural world, as if it had a family, just as you do. How is this family of beings threatened or dominated by the members of our human family? What is their history? How are they resisting or adapting to the threats they face? How does this knowledge land in your body?

If you were a member of their family (and you are), how would you want to see them treated? What can you do to support their liberation and freedom from ongoing threat and harm? And in those cases where an element of the natural world feels more powerful than you are, how do you feel in your body in response to that power?

7

Bringing It All Home

We were simply trying to change the way we went about our everyday lives so that our values and habits of being would reflect our commitment to freedom.[1]

—BELL HOOKS

In this final chapter of *Embodied Activism,* we bring together the ideas and practices described in previous chapters and apply them to an everyday activism that manifests in our bodies, our relationships, our communities, and our world. We begin by identifying the areas of social and political life that matter most to us, and then we connect those commitments to our singular gifts and to collective needs. Even those of us who have been in social justice spaces for many years can benefit from a thoughtful realignment of our purpose with our passions.

As always, our bodies are an essential resource in helping us find pathways for our actions that support our ongoing resilience. As Audre Lorde noted, caring for ourselves is not self-indulgence but self-preservation, and any action that allows us to thrive and to live deeply and fully in our own skins is a radical political act.[2] Finding our honest, embodied capacities for the work is essential for activism that is sustainable—activism that refuses to perpetuate worn-out stereotypes of activist well-being as something that is somehow dispensable in service to a greater good. This chapter offers a framework for assessing our capacities and navigating the demands of our political work so that we don't sacrifice our bodies to our causes.

This chapter also offers recommendations for further exploration of embodied activism, including information on community resources, specialized training programs, and educational events. Although the exploration of how our bodies can become forces for change can be deeply personal, this work always necessarily occurs in the context of relationship and community. The section on community connections is intended to help readers get plugged into the networks, forums, and platforms that can help them thrive.

Finding Our Grooves and Mapping Our Assets

There are as many ways of engaging in activism as there are activists willing to do the work. Earlier in this book, I noted Deepa Iyer's framework for identifying the various roles in a social change ecosystem.[3] Beyond the roles that Iyer describes (healer, weaver, storyteller, and frontline responder, for example) we can easily add artist, researcher, teacher, and many more. There's room for everyone in an embodied activism: introverts and extroverts, parents and kids, and folks who don't necessarily follow politics but who feel injustice when they come across it. Regardless of our background, our education, or our position in life, we all have some power to make the world—our world—a better place. The question is, where in our lives will we choose to take a stand? And what leverage do we have available to us?

This is where an exercise called *asset mapping* can be helpful. Asset mapping is a process frequently used in community planning to identify the existing individual, group, and community resources that can be put to work in a project. By definition, an asset map focuses on what we *have* rather than on what we need. It is a tool for identifying and visualizing our current capacities. Asset maps can take many forms, but their purpose is underscoring our strengths, tangible and intangible, so we can harness them toward a particular goal. While asset maps are most often employed in the context of communities, individuals can also usefully engage in asset mapping.[4] Individual assets might include our passions, talents, expertise, knowledge, and resources.

On a body level, asset maps become a way to visualize more concretely how we might embody our activism. The asset map won't tell us what to do, but it can help us realize the embodied talents and skills we possess so we can put those assets to work. For those who are new to activism, an asset map can provide a sense that we have something concrete to offer. For seasoned activists, it can offer a way to cross-check our social justice work against our existing resources to make sure we're offering something that's aligned with our current capacities. Because our resources change over time, doing an asset map can provide a fresh read on what we're doing so we can respond to the imbalances that can lead to burnout.

EMBODIED PRAXIS
Creating an Embodied Asset Map

Take a moment to check in with yourself on a body level. Maybe take a few easy, comfortable breaths, close your eyes, and settle into your seat or onto the floor.

- When you think about the changes you want to see in the world, where do your passions lie? What gets you fired up? Where do you feel those enthusiasms in your body?

- What affinities, talents, or gifts do you bring? Do you have special expertise or knowledge you can offer? Where do you feel these in your body?

- What resources can you devote to your activism? Are you privileged or positioned in ways that might be leveraged to support others?

When you've had a chance to feel into how these assets land in your body, draw an outline of your body on a sheet of paper and map your assets onto it. Once you've created your embodied asset map, consider how you might match the assets you possess with the needs of a particular community or cause. If you're already engaged in activism, use your asset map to check for alignment with what you're doing, what you're good at, and what you're realistically able to offer.

Aligning Our Embodied Capacities
with the Work

One of the challenges of working to change the world is that it's almost always *hard* work, even when it's deeply rewarding. And typically, this hard work is taken up by those who suffer the most from the injustices embedded into oppressive social systems. It's easy to get worn down and worn out, especially if others are counting on us. For most of us, maintaining a sense of resilience—the capacity to bounce back and keep going—is crucial. But what if resilience is not a kind of toughness that automatically happens to us when we endure something hard or demanding? What if true resilience asks us to access and respond to how we're feeling in our bodies so we can adapt to new challenges?

In much the same way that cultivating a broad somatic bandwidth helps us navigate difficult situations, our overall resilience also entails a certain kind of bandwidth. Our ability to sustain ourselves (and, by extension, our communities) requires that we assess and address our capacity for ongoing work. Yet our capacities are not the same as everyone else's, and they change over time. One day we may have ample strength and endurance for resisting and risking. Other days we can barely contemplate the struggle, much less engage in it. We might have lots of energy for physical tasks and little heart for emotional labor. Perhaps we are tapped out relationally but are happy to work quietly in a corner on a mundane administrative task. Being responsive to our changing needs for rest and for challenge is key to sustainable embodied activism.

If we think of our overall well-being as existing on a continuum, we might imagine a central point of balance where we feel engaged, alive, and energized by the challenges we face, not just because these challenges are meaningful to us but because we have the resources (both internal and external) to meet those challenges. The balance between demands and resources is just right. Yet, when we lose resources (or the demands upon us increase), how we feel in our body shifts. We might begin to feel stressed, unhappy, tired, or overwhelmed. Our hearts might race, or it could feel hard to catch a full breath. Over time, our body will start to feel the negative effects of this chronic imbalance, wearing down and showing stress fractures such as illness or irritability.

Yet our bodies are remarkably responsive to changes in environmental conditions. A simple reduction in demands or an increase in resources can quickly shift how we feel. We begin to move back toward the center of the continuum. The resources we add can be simple ones: getting a hug, taking a nap, having a good meal, or getting some fresh air. Other times, the resources we need are more complex and harder to put in place, such as childcare, health care, or a steady income. Either way, the math still works: when we're feeling exhausted or overwhelmed, adding resources and/or reducing demands will help shift the feeling in our bodies and allow our batteries to recharge themselves. Of course, this doesn't mean we approach our resilience in a calculated, mechanistic way; rather, we *feel* into what's needed using our sensibilities around balance and imbalance to guide us. What are we craving when we take time to listen to our body?

Interestingly, the imbalance between demands and resources can also show up as the result of a sustained period of too many resources and too few demands. When this kind of imbalance is present in our lives, the feeling in our body can turn to listlessness, boredom, and apathy. We begin to crave a challenge, perhaps becoming more inclined to take risks or pick a fight. In these situations, the solution is often to find healthy challenges and to share our resources with others.

Either way, it's helpful to learn how to 1) identify the feeling in our bodies that lets us know we're out of balance (stressed or bored), 2) identify our current demands and resources, and 3) tweak the balance by adding resources or subtracting demands as needed. Adjusting this balance can help us become more resilient.

EMBODIED PRAXIS
Creating an Embodied Resilience Map

On a sheet of paper, map out five sections, one each for the 1) physical, 2) emotional, 3) relational, 4) intellectual, and 5) spiritual domains of your life.[5] You can change the names of these domains so they suit you, or you might want to combine several or add some new ones. Although these domains may appear distinct and separate on the surface, they're all facets of our somatic experience; that is, we experience all of them on a body level. The actual names of the domains (or where they might converge or overlap) aren't particularly important. The idea is to begin to tease out where some of your demands and resources show up in your life right now. As you consider the demands you experience, notice that some of them might be internal demands, that is, expectations you have of yourself. Resources can also be internal, such as patience or a sense of humor. Consider both external and internal demands and resources in each of these domains:

1. On a physical level, what's hard on your body in your life right now? What's draining or painful? Maybe it's sitting at a computer all day or standing behind a counter. What's sustaining or nourishing? What helps your body bounce back or feel good? Perhaps a long, quiet run or some

passionate lovemaking. Perhaps simply tuning into your senses or taking a breath. Think of the energy boosters that work for you on a body level, large and small.

2. On an emotional level, what's hurting your heart right now? What's draining or distressing emotionally? Are you awash in feelings that are hard to bear? On the other hand, what helps your heart sing? What helps ease your heart's burden, even just for a while?

3. On a relational level, what's tough in your life right now? Where in your body do you feel those relational gaps or challenges? Who in your life feels like a source of sustenance or nourishment? What relationships help you feel alive and connected these days? Note them all, even the seemingly insignificant ones. (See Danusha Laméris's poem "Small Kindnesses" in the previous chapter for a reminder of the importance of counting all the ways that our relationships—human and more-than-human—help make life worth living.) Map the impact of these relational gifts on your body.

4. On an intellectual or psychological level, what's demanding or taxing? What kinds of cognitive tasks wear you out or drag you down? What kinds of intellectual activities are stimulating and invigorating? What helps your brain feel rested and alive?

5. On a spiritual level, what's hard right now? What kinds of things feel draining or demoralizing to your soul? On the other hand, are there sources of comfort, joy, or inspiration in your life that feel sustaining or nourishing on a spiritual level?

Once you've completed your embodied resilience map, look at how the demands and resources balance out on paper. Does the map help you make better sense of how you're feeling and what you might do to help shift the balance between the demands and resources in your life? Are you able to identify any hidden drains on your energy or places where you experience extraordinary demands? Are there a lot of resources bunched up in just one area, with few resources in the other domains of your life?

On your map, highlight any current demands you might want to consider refusing, redirecting, delaying, or spreading out into an easier load. Likewise, highlight any underutilized resources that you might draw on more often, as well as any reliable resources that could serve as your go-to strategies for when you're feeling stressed or upset. Put the map in a place where it's easy to access when you're feeling overwhelmed and need ideas for how to support your body in acting on its natural impulse toward balance. Update your map as you learn more about what works for you, as the demands and resources in your life change.

An Integrative Framework for Everyday Embodied Activism

The foundation of an embodied activism is to cultivate the somatic capacities to challenge, resist, and transform unjust power dynamics as they manifest in the context of our everyday lives. Sometimes, these dynamics will emerge spontaneously during our body-to-body interactions with others, and we'll need to improvise a response by drawing on existing skills and strategies. This is often the case with embodied microaggressions and asymmetrical nonverbal communication, as discussed in earlier chapters. Other times, the injustices are more entrenched—contexts where we can reasonably expect to encounter the systemic misuse of power on a regular basis. In other words, there's a role for in-the-moment, spontaneous actions as well as for more strategic and proactive interventions. The following framework is designed to help us view our embodied interventions in a more integrated way, helping us connect the dots between our values and our actions and giving us a better sense of how what we're doing adds up.

Using the composite hypothetical example of an activist named Jackson, the framework maps an overall strategy of embodied activism across several domains. The top row outlines three strategies that Jackson currently uses to support their own (and others) embodied liberation. In this example, these three strategies are 1) disrupting gender norms, 2) reclaiming sensuality, and 3) supporting ecological sustainability, but the specific strategies will be different for everyone. Other strategies might be honoring Black cultures, making autism more visible, or supporting embodied resilience among the elderly. What the strategies look like will depend on each person's particular interests, capacities, and commitments.

	STRATEGY 1: DISRUPTING EMBODIED GENDER NORMS	STRATEGY 2: RECLAIMING SENSUALITY	STRATEGY 3: SUPPORTING ECOLOGICAL SUSTAINABILITY
The social forces this strategy resists, disrupts, or transforms	Cisheteronormativity Imposed gender binaries	Puritanism Industrialization Body objectification and commodification	Capitalism Consumerism Anthrocentrism
Examples of how this strategy is being enacted through body image	Wearing clothes assigned to both genders simultaneously—a suit jacket with a skirt, for example Wearing a beard and make-up together	Clothes that are soft, movable, and unrestricting Going barefoot indoors Not wearing a tie	Wearing recycled, second-hand, or sustainably produced clothing
Examples of how this strategy is being enacted through diet		Preparing fragrant, flavorful, home-cooked food Taking time to taste, smell, and enjoy food	Eating organic, local, fair trade, and ethically produced food Not wasting food
Examples of how this strategy is being enacted through nonverbal communication and movement practices	Gestures that cross gender norms, such as sitting with ankles crossed and hands folded in lap, or using soft, flowing movements	Engaging in expressive movement, touch, and breathwork	Using walking as a primary mode of transport
Examples of how this strategy is being enacted through community praxis	Donating money to the Trans Clippers Project Organizing an embodiment group at a local Pride organization	Advocating for a barefoot policy at the preschool where they work	Starting a community garden

Jackson began by reflecting on (and then writing down) some of the little things they were doing on an everyday basis that felt like embodied resistance or transformation in some way. Jackson then arranged these activities into groups of things that felt like they belonged together in some way. Once the groups were formed, it was possible to see the links from their everyday efforts to the larger oppressive social forces at work (the second row on the chart). Also, by grouping individual examples in this way, Jackson was able to see how small efforts add up and where they might be doing more to resist a particular ideological colonization into the intimate spaces of their flesh and bone.

Looking at the groupings, Jackson then made note of all the places in their life where their commitments to genderqueerness, sensuality, and sustainability were currently manifesting. Because of Jackson's natural affinity for working with their body image, it was one of the biggest places where their acts of resistance were focused. Of course, for someone for whom clothes and grooming are not such a big deal, this section might not even appear on their chart. In Jackson's case, they also added diet and movement practices to their map, which helped to coalesce the work they were already doing as a yoga instructor and organic gardener. As a yoga instructor, Jackson was viscerally aware of how movement shapes their sense of their body and how moving helps them metabolize the environmental toxins of oppression. As an organic gardener, Jackson was also attentive to the ways in which the food they eat supports or fails to support the kind of world and the kind of body they want to live in. Finally, Jackson included examples of everyday embodied activism that extended beyond the personal and relational realms and into the community. This fourth category in the first column gave Jackson space to map examples of how each strategy—disrupting gender norms, reclaiming sensuality, and supporting ecological sustainability—was also being enacted through their work with others.

When using this integrative framework to help think through your own embodied activism, it's important to keep in mind that frameworks are only a guide to organizing a bottom-up process of sensing and perceiving what your body and your community might need to feel more healed and liberated. There's no right or wrong way to create the details of your own framework—just a desire to see how the everyday little things really do add up, and a commitment to align those activities with the larger changes we want to see in the world. Hopefully, working with this framework will help make more visible how the personal is political on a body level, and will affirm that many of our embodied impulses toward justice are often neither random nor unstrategic, after all. And of course, mapping our embodied activism in this way helps us see where we might do more.

Perhaps the most useful aspect of an integrative framework for embodied activism is how it can help us identify where we want to go, not just where we are. In some cases, taking the next step on our path is as simple as identifying it, such as making more time for a personal movement practice or reaching out to a particular community group to offer our time, energy, and resources. Other times, it can be harder to identify exactly how to go about the embodied activism we want to manifest. This is where plugging into larger networks of activity and learning can be helpful.

Community Resources

As we commit to the cultivation of our own capacities as engaged and embodied beings who recognize the impact of oppression on our own bodies, we also undertake to heal and prevent the personal and relational damage that occurs in oppressive social systems. Doing our own work allows us to work with others with integrity and offers us some protection from burnout by helping us reconnect with our bodies as a source of knowledge and power. This section offers information and links to current resources that readers might find helpful in further developing their knowledge and skill in embodied activism.[6]

The section is divided into the following categories:

- **Embodied coaching, counseling, and therapy resources** for those wanting specialized support on their own journey of healing and liberation
- **Educational and training resources** for those wanting to cultivate personal or professional skills in relation to embodied activism
- **Embodied writing resources**
- **Conferences and summits** that offer community events on the topics of embodied social justice and activism
- **Reading list** of related books, articles, and videos

Embodied Coaching, Counseling, and Therapy Resources

The following professional organizations provide a searchable list of accredited professional members with expertise in somatic practices. Refining your search and/or reviewing individual practitioner bios will identify those who also bring a social justice perspective to their work.

INTERNATIONAL SOMATIC MOVEMENT EDUCATION AND
THERAPY ASSOCIATION
www.ismeta.org/locate-a-practitioner#!directory/map/ord=lnm

UNITED STATES ASSOCIATION OF BODY PSYCHOTHERAPY
www.usabp.org/Find-a-Therapist

EUROPEAN ASSOCIATION OF BODY PSYCHOTHERAPY
www.eabp.org/find-a-therapist/

AMERICAN DANCE THERAPY ASSOCIATION
www.adta.org/find-a-dmt#/

Educational and Training Resources

The organizations listed in this section offer training and education using approaches that integrate the body with trauma, conflict, and/or social justice.

CULTURAL SOMATICS TRAINING INSTITUTE
www.culturalsomaticsinstitute.com/courses

> A collection of embodied knowledge courses that empower you to develop embodied racial literacy so you can develop a life and community centered on abolishing White body supremacy.

EMBODY DEEP DEMOCRACY
www.embodydeepdemocracy.com

> Aims to bring deeper awareness and engagement to feeling, imagination, ancestors, and spiritual knowing; an intelligence that precedes experiences of colonization, apartheid, or oppression.

EMBODY PEACE

www.embodypeace.wordpress.com

> Connecting organizations and individuals who engage in peacemaking through the embodied arts, movement, and body awareness.

EMBODIED ACTIVISM

www.embodiedphilosophy.com/embodied-activism-navigating-the
-intersections-of-embodiment-social-justice

> An evergreen online course on embodied activism with Nkem Ndefo and Rae Johnson, offered through the online educational platform Embody Lab.

EMBODIED LIBERATION

www.embodiedliberation.com

> Dedicated to offering ideas, writing, workshops, and unequivocal encouragement as we navigate the intensity of the tensions between terror and safety, oppression and justice, and love and liberation.

EMBODIED SOCIAL JUSTICE

www.embodiedsocialjustice.com

> Provides coaching, training, and consultation to organizations, agencies, and schools on the approach to embodied activism outlined in this book.

EMBODIED SOCIAL JUSTICE CERTIFICATE PROGRAM

www.transformativechange.org

> Transformative Change offers an Embodied Social Justice certificate, a three-month online program that explores how we embody unjust social conditions, how oppression affects our relationship with our body, and how we can harness the body's wisdom in making our social justice work more grounded, responsive, and sustainable.

GENERATIVE SOMATICS

www.generativesomatics.org

> Offers training in a form of politicized somatics that draws on embodied practices to create social change by linking individual experiences of trauma to the social contexts in which we live.

INTERNATIONAL FOCUSING INSTITUTE
www.focusing.org

An international, cross-cultural organization dedicated to supporting individuals and groups worldwide who are practicing, teaching, and developing Focusing and its underlying philosophy.

INTERPLAY
www.interplay.org

Offers workshop intensives on embodiment and racism called Changing the Race Dance, creating a space for participants to "engage in empowering opportunities to address race and racism and unpack inequity with fewer words and more wisdom."

JUST ACT
www.justact.org

Just Act is an applied theater nonprofit organization committed to and trained in artistic activism. It offers multilevel training in Theatre of the Oppressed techniques for those embarking on a journey or who want to go deeper with their practice and self-understanding within an antioppression framework.

MOVING ON CENTER
www.movingoncenter.org

A training program linking somatics and the performing arts for social change. Using experiential and cooperative learning, Moving on Center has a mission to develop community leaders and artists who engage the whole bodymind to promote holistic social change.

OFF THE MAT INTO THE WORLD
www.offthematintotheworld.org

A community of leaders bridging the tools of yoga with sustainable, conscious activism and effective community action on and off the mat.

SINS INVALID
www.sinsinvalid.org/creative-workshops

Sins Invalid is a disability justice–based performance project that incubates and celebrates artists with disabilities, centralizing artists of color and LGBTQIA+/gender-variant artists as communities who have been historically marginalized. Sins Invalid offers accessible creative workshops for universities, organizations, and community members.

SOMATIC EXPERIENCING INTERNATIONAL
www.traumahealing.org/anti-oppression-resources

Dedicated to supporting trauma resolution and resilience through culturally responsive professional training and education, research, and outreach around the globe. Provides training in Somatic Experiencing, antioppression resources (see link above), and a practitioner directory.

STREET DANCE ACTIVISM
www.streetdanceactivism.com

Offers a daily practice app, street dance activation workshops, and radical embodiment talks with leading Black choreographers.

Embodied Writing Resources

Here are two resources specially focused on embodied writing, for readers wanting additional support and inspiration for writing their body story.

SOMATIC WRITING
www.somaticwriting.com/about

Somatic Writing is a body-centered creative process to support you in writing, speaking, and integrating your story. Founder and director Tanya Taylor Rubinstein developed Somatic Writing as a way for her students to become embodied writers. By holistically retrieving voice, untethering power, and writing stories, they can experience profound personal connection to their work.

WRITING FROM THE BODY
www.paulajosajones.org

Paula Josa Jones offers workshops for "movers who think they can't write and writers who think they can't move." Weaving together improvisational movement practices with spontaneous writing, her workshops offer participants strategies for finding words to take from the body to the page and off the page into the body.

Conferences and Summits

BODY IQ SOMATICS FESTIVAL: BODIES OF CULTURES, COMMUNITIES, AND PLACES
www.bodyiq.berlin

> The Body IQ Festival aims to address questions of embodied recovery and revisioning in the context of global ethical, social, and ecological crises and change. Somatic practices have moved beyond a field of sensorial, experiential, and emancipatory learning into wider educational, therapeutic, artistic and social-justice contexts.

DANCING RESILIENCE: DANCE STUDIES AND ACTIVISM IN A GLOBAL AGE
www.dancestudiesassociation.org

> An annual conference that convenes presenters to explore dance and activism in localized and transcultural settings and to share their strategies for productive change on the stage, street, and screen and within the academy.

EMBODIED SOCIAL JUSTICE SUMMIT
www.embodiedsocialjusticesummit.com

> The Embodied Social Justice Summit is dedicated to exploring the intersection of oppression and embodiment: how social and political structures are embedded within bodies and how through engaging the body we can respond to the social justice issues of our time and begin the work of dismantling oppressive systems.

ENGAGING EMBODIMENT: SOMATIC APPLICATIONS FOR HEALTH, EDUCATION, AND SOCIAL JUSTICE
www.ismeta.org/engaging-embodiment-conference-2#!form

Reading List

This list offers books and articles that deal with many of the topics introduced in *Embodied Activism*. Some of these readings have already been cited in the text, but this is not a complete reference list. Please consult the endnotes for full references to sources cited in the text. Most articles listed in this section are open access and do not require a subscription to an academic journal.

Abram, David. "Becoming Animal." *Green Letters* 13, no. 1 (2010): 7–21.

Abram, David. *The Spell of the Sensuous: Perception and Language in a More-Than-Human World.* New York: Vintage, 2012.

Ackerman, Diane. *Deep Play.* New York: Vintage, 2011.

Ackerman, Diane. *A Natural History of the Senses.* New York: Vintage, 1991.

Akomolafe, Bayo. *These Wilds Beyond Our Fences: Letters to My Daughter on Humanity's Search for Home.* Berkeley, CA: North Atlantic Books, 2017.

Allen, Shaonta, and Brittney Miles. "Unapologetic Blackness in Action: Embodied Resistance and Social Movement Scenes in Black Celebrity Activism." *Humanity and Society* 44, no. 4 (2020): 375–402.

Allen, Wendy. "The Somatic Experience of White Privilege: A Dance/Movement Therapy Approach to Racialized Interactions." Ph.D. diss., Lesley University, 2018. https://digitalcommons.lesley.edu/expressive_dissertations/59/.

Anderson, Rosemarie. "Embodied Writing: Presencing the Body in Somatic Research, Part I: What Is Embodied Writing?" *Somatics* 13, no. 4 (2002): 40–44.

Archer, Dane. "Unspoken Diversity: Cultural Differences in Gestures." *Qualitative Sociology* 20, no. 1 (1997): 79–105. https://link.springer.com/article/10.1023/A:1024716331692.

Argyle, Michael. *Bodily Communication.* New York: Routledge, 2013.

Atkins, Dawn. *Looking Queer: Body Image and Identity in Lesbian, Bisexual, Gay, and Transgender Communities.* New York: Routledge, 2012.

Aviezer, Hillel, Yaacov Trope, and Alexander Todorov. "Body Cues, Not Facial Expressions, Discriminate between Intense Positive and Negative Emotions." *Science* 338, no. 6111 (2012): 1225–29.

Batacharya, S., and Wong, Y. L. R., eds. *Sharing Breath: Embodied Learning and Decolonization.* Athabasca, AB: Athabasca University Press, 2018.

Bauer, Susan. *The Embodied Teen: A Somatic Curriculum for Teaching Body-Mind Awareness, Kinesthetic Intelligence, and Social and Emotional Skills.* Berkeley, CA: North Atlantic Books, 2018.

Bergman, Carla, and Nick Montgomery. *Joyful Militancy: Building Thriving Resistance in Toxic Times.* Oakland, CA: AK Press, 2017.

Bell, Shamell Andria Janette. "Living is Resisting: An Autoethnography and Oral History of Street Dance Activism in Los Angeles." Ph.D. diss., University of California, Los Angeles, 2019.

Berila, Beth. *Integrating Mindfulness into Anti-Oppression Pedagogy: Social Justice in Higher Education*. New York: Routledge, 2015.

Berila, Beth. *Radiating Feminism: Resilience Practices to Transform Our Inner and Outer Lives*. New York: Routledge, 2020.

Bobel, Chris, and Samantha Kwan, eds. *Embodied Resistance: Challenging the Norms, Breaking the Rules*. Nashville, TN: Vanderbilt University Press, 2011.

Bourdieu, Pierre. "Structures, Habitus, Practices." In *Rethinking the Subject,* edited by James Faubion, 31–45. New York: Routledge, 2018.

Brown, Adrienne Maree. *Pleasure Activism: The Politics of Feeling Good*. Oakland, CA: AK Press, 2019.

Bryant-Davis, Thema, and Carlota Ocampo. "Racist Incident–Based Trauma." *Counseling Psychologist* 33, no. 4 (2005): 479–500.

Burgoon, Judee K., Valerie Manusov, and Laura K. Guerrero. *Nonverbal Communication*. New York: Routledge, 2021.

Butler, Judith. *Bodies That Matter: On the Discursive Limits of Sex*. New York: Routledge, 2011.

Caine, Vera, Pam Steeves, D. Jean Clandinin, Andrew Estefan, Janice Huber, and M. Shaun Murphy. "Social Justice Practice: A Narrative Inquiry Perspective." *Education, Citizenship and Social Justice* 13, no. 2 (2018): 133–43.

Caldwell, Christine. "Diversity Issues in Movement Observation and Assessment." *American Journal of Dance Therapy* 35 (2013): 183–200. doi.org/10.1007/s10465-013-9159-9.

Caldwell, Christine, and Lucia Bennett Leighton, eds. *Oppression and the Body: Roots, Resistance, and Resolutions*. Berkeley, CA: North Atlantic Books, 2018.

Carter, Robert T. "Racism and Psychological and Emotional Injury: Recognizing and Assessing Race-Based Traumatic Stress." *Counseling Psychologist* 35, no. 1 (2007): 13–105.

Carvalho, Gil B., and Antonio Damasio. "Interoception and the Origin of Feelings: A New Synthesis." *BioEssays* 43, no. 6 (2021): https://doi.org/10.1002/bies.202000261.

Chugh, Dolly. *The Person You Mean to Be: How Good People Fight Bias*. New York: HarperBusiness, 2018.

Clare, Eli. "Body Shame, Body Pride: Lessons from the Disability Rights Movement." In *The Transgender Studies Reader,* edited by Susan Stryker and S. Whittle, 261–65. London: Routledge, 2013.

Clare, Eli. "Stolen Bodies, Reclaimed Bodies: Disability and Queerness." *Public Culture* 13, no. 3 (2001): 359–65.

Cohen, Bonnie Bainbridge, Lisa Nelson, and Nancy Stark Smith. *Sensing, Feeling, and Action: The Experiential Anatomy of Body-Mind Centering.* Middlebury, CT: Contact Editions, 2012.

Cohen, Jerome J., and Gail Weiss, eds. *Thinking the Limits of the Body.* Buffalo: State University of New York Press, 2012.

Cooper, Mick. "Embodied Empathy." In *Empathy,* edited by S. Haugh and T. Merry, 218–29. Ross-on-Wye: PCCS Books, 2001.

Cottom, Tressie McMillan. *Thick: And Other Essays.* New York: The New Press, 2018.

Craig, Arthur D. "How Do You Feel? Interoception: The Sense of the Physiological Condition of the Body." *Nature Reviews Neuroscience* 3, no. 8 (2002): 655–66.

Crenshaw, Kimberlé W. *On Intersectionality: Essential Writings.* New York: The New Press, 2017.

Csikszentmihalyi, Mihaly, Sami Abuhamdeh, and Jeanne Nakamura. "Flow." In *Flow and the Foundations of Positive Psychology,* 227–38. New York: Springer, 2014.

Csordas, Thomas. *Embodiment and Experience: The Existential Ground of Culture and Self.* Cambridge, UK: Cambridge University Press, 1994.

Drew, Lara. "Embodied Learning Processes in Activism." *Canadian Journal for the Study of Adult Education (Online)* 27, no. 1 (2014): 83. https://cjsae .library.dal.ca/index.php/cjsae/article/view/3410.

Edut, Ophira. *Body Outlaws: Rewriting the Rules of Beauty and Body Image.* Emeryville, CA: Seal Press, 2014.

Ellyson, Steve L., and John F. Dovidio, eds. *Power, Dominance, and Nonverbal Behavior.* New York: Springer, 2012.

Fahs, Breanne. "Dreaded 'Otherness': Heteronormative Patrolling in Women's Body Hair Rebellions." *Gender and Society* 25, no. 4 (2011): 451–72.

Farb, Norman, and Wolf E. Mehling. "Interoception, Contemplative Practice, and Health." *Frontiers in Psychology* 7 (2016): 1898.

Fidyk, A. "Body Maps as Ecological, Affective, Relational and Decolonizing Method." *Journal of the Canadian Association for Curriculum Studies* 18, no. 1 (2020): 123–26.

Freire, Paulo. *Pedagogy of the Oppressed.* New York: Continuum, 2000.

Gendlin, Eugene. *Focusing.* New York: Bantam, 1982.

Gilbert, Paul, and Jeremy Miles. *Body Shame: Conceptualisation, Research and Treatment.* New York: Routledge, 2014.

Grogan, Sarah. *Body Image: Understanding Body Dissatisfaction in Men, Women, and Children.* New York: Routledge, 2021.

Haines, Staci K. *The Politics of Trauma: Somatics, Healing, and Social Justice.* Berkeley, CA: North Atlantic Books, 2019.

Hanna, Thomas. *Bodies in Revolt: A Primer in Somatic Thinking.* Novato, CA: Freeperson Press, 1970.

Hardy, Emma. "Queer Aesthetics: Not Feeling Queer Enough." *Archer,* April 11, 2017. http://archermagazine.com.au/2017/04/queer-aesthetics-not-feeling-queer-enough/.

Haselager, Willem Ferdinand Garardus, Mariana Cláudia Broens, and Maria Eunice Quilici Gonzalez. "The Importance of Sensing One's Movement in the World for the Sense of Personal Identity." *Rivista internazionale di Filosofia e Psicologia* 3, no. 1 (2012): 1–11.

Hervey, Lenore W. "Embodied Ethical Decision Making." *American Journal of Dance Therapy* 29, no. 2 (2007): 91–108.

hooks, bell. *Teaching to Transgress.* New York: Routledge, 2014.

Johnson, Allan. *Power, Privilege, and Difference.* Mountain View, CA: Mayfield Publishing, 2001.

Johnson, Don Hanlon, ed. *Diverse Bodies, Diverse Practices: Toward an Inclusive Somatics.* Berkeley, CA: North Atlantic Books, 2018.

Johnson, Rae. *Embodied Social Justice.* New York: Routledge, 2017.

Johnson, Rae. "Grasping and Transforming the Embodied Experience of Oppression." *International Body Psychotherapy Journal* 14, no. 1 (2015): 80–95.

Johnson, Rae. *Knowing in Our Bones: Exploring the Embodied Knowledge of Somatic Educators.* Saarbrucken: Lambert Academic Publishing, 2001.

Johnson, Rae, Lucia Leighton, and Christine Caldwell. "The Embodied Experience of Microaggressions: Implications for Clinical Practice." *Journal of Multicultural Counseling and Development* 46, no. 3 (2018): 156–70.

Kimpson, Sally A. "Embodied Activism: Constructing a Transgressive Self." 2001. https://kb.osu.edu/bitstream/handle/1811/85554/DSQ_v20n3_2000_319.pdf.

Knaster, Mirka. *Discovering the Body's Wisdom.* New York: Bantam Books, 1996.

Kolb, Alice Y., and David A. Kolb. "Experiential Learning Theory." In *Encyclopedia of the Sciences of Learning*. Thousand Oaks, CA: Sage, 2012.

Kumashiro, Kevin K. *Against Common Sense: Teaching and Learning toward Social Justice*. New York: Routledge, 2013.

LaFrance, Marianne. "Smile Boycotts and Other Body Politics." *Feminism and Psychology* 12, no. 3 (2002): 319–23.

Levine, Peter A. *In an Unspoken Voice: How the Body Releases Trauma and Restores Goodness*. Berkeley, CA: North Atlantic Books, 2010.

Lorde, Audre. *Burst of Light*. London: Women's Press, 1992.

Lewin, Miche Fabre. "Liberation and the Art of Embodiment." In *Revisiting Feminist Approaches to Art Therapy*, edited by Susan Hogan, 140–48. New York: Berghahn Books, 2012.

Maine, Margo. *Body Wars: Making Peace with Women's Bodies*. Carlsbad, CA: Gurze Books, 2011.

Mazon, Mauricio. *The Zoot-Suit Riots: The Psychology of Symbolic Annihilation*. Austin: University of Texas Press, 2002.

McIntosh, Peggy. "White Privilege: Unpacking the Invisible Knapsack." In *Race, Class, and Gender in the United States: An Integrated Study*, edited by Paula S. Rothenberg, 177–82. New York: Worth Publishers, 2007.

McRuer, Robert. *Desiring Disability: Queer Theory Meets Disability Studies*. Durham, NC: Duke University Press, 2007.

Menakem, Resmaa. *My Grandmother's Hands: Racialized Trauma and the Pathway to Mending Our Hearts and Bodies*. New York: Penguin Books, 2021.

Merleau-Ponty, Maurice. *Phenomenology of Perception*. New York: Routledge, 1962.

Meyer, Christian, Jürgen Streeck, and J. Scott Jordan, eds. *Intercorporeality: Emerging Socialities in Interaction*. New York: Oxford University Press, 2017.

Mills, Dana. *Dance and Activism: A Century of Radical Dance across the World*. London: Bloomsbury Publishing, 2021.

Mol, Saskia, Arnoud Arntz, Job F. M. Metsemakers, Geert-Jan Dinant, Pauline A. P. Vilters-Van Montfort, and J. André Knottnerus. "Symptoms of Post-Traumatic Stress Disorder after Non-traumatic Events: Evidence from an Open Population Study." *British Journal of Psychiatry* 186, no. 6 (2005): 494–99.

Ngo, Helen. *The Habits of Racism: A Phenomenology of Racism and Racialized Embodiment*. Washington, DC: Lexington Books, 2017.

Noland, Carrie. *Agency and Embodiment*. Cambridge, MA: Harvard University Press, 2010.

Ogden, Pat, Kekuni Minton, and Clare Pain. *Trauma and the Body: A Sensorimotor Approach to Psychotherapy*. New York: W. W. Norton, 2006.

Pease, Bob. *Undoing Privilege: Unearned Advantage in a Divided World*. London: Bloomsbury Publishing, 2010.

Piepzna-Samarasinha, Leah Lakshmi. *Care Work: Dreaming Disability Justice*. Vancouver, BC: Arsenal Pulp Press, 2018.

Porges, Stephen W. *The Polyvagal Theory: Neurophysiological Foundations of Emotions, Attachment, Communication, and Self-Regulation*. New York: W. W. Norton, 2011.

Sapon-Shevin, Mara, and Suzanne SooHoo. "Embodied Social Justice Pedagogy in a Time of 'No Touch.'" *Postdigital Science and Education* 2, no. 3 (2020): 675–80.

Selvam, Raja. *The Practice of Embodying Emotions*. Berkeley, CA: North Atlantic Books, 2022.

Shilling, Chris. *The Body and Social Theory*. Thousand Oaks, CA: Sage, 2012.

Siegel, Daniel. Developing Mind: How Relationships and the Brain Interact to Shape Who We Are. New York: Guilford Press, 2012.

Singh, Anneliese A. *The Queer and Transgender Resilience Workbook: Skills for Navigating Sexual Orientation and Gender Expression*. Oakland, CA: New Harbinger Publications, 2018.

Stone, Douglas, Bruce Patton, and Sheila Heen. *Difficult Conversations: How to Discuss What Matters Most*. New York: Penguin, 2010.

Sue, Derald Wing. *Microaggressions in Everyday Life: Race, Gender, and Sexual Orientation*. Hoboken, NJ: John Wiley & Sons, 2010.

Sue, Derald Wing, Cassandra Z. Calle, Narolyn Mendez, Sarah Alsaidi, and Elizabeth Glaeser. *Microintervention Strategies: What You Can Do to Disarm and Dismantle Individual and Systemic Racism and Bias*. Hoboken, NJ: John Wiley & Sons, 2020.

Sullivan, Nikki. *A Critical Introduction to Queer Theory*. New York: New York University Press, 2003.

Taylor, Sonya Renee. *The Body Is Not an Apology: The Power of Radical Self-Love*. Oakland, CA: Berrett-Koehler Publishers, 2021.

Tsakiris, Manos. "The Multisensory Basis of the Self: From Body to Identity to Others." *Quarterly Journal of Experimental Psychology* 70, no. 4 (2017): 597–609.

Turner, Bryan S. *The Body and Society: Explorations in Social Theory*. Thousand Oaks, CA: Sage, 2008.

Van der Kolk, Bessel A. *The Body Keeps the Score: Brain, Mind, and Body in the Healing of Trauma*. New York: Penguin Books, 2015.

Weber, Andreas. *The Biology of Wonder: Aliveness, Feeling and the Metamorphosis of Science*. Gabriola Island, BC: New Society Publishers, 2016.

Weiss, Gail. *Body Images: Embodiment as Intercorporeality*. New York: Routledge, 2013.

Westland, Gill. *Verbal and Nonverbal Communication in Psychotherapy*. New York: W. W. Norton, 2015.

Wilcox, Hui Niu. "Embodied Ways of Knowing, Pedagogies, and Social Justice: Inclusive Science and Beyond." *NWSA Journal* 21, no. 2 (2009): 104–20.

Young, Iris Marion. "Throwing Like a Girl: A Phenomenology of Feminine Body Comportment Motility and Spatiality." *Human Studies* 3, no. 1 (1980): 137–56.

Yuasa, Yasuo. *The Body: Toward an Eastern Mind-Body Theory*. Albany: SUNY Press, 1987.

Notes

1. Reconsidering, Reframing, and Retooling

1 Pinkwashing refers to a strategy of "rainbow capitalism" that involves targeted marketing to an increasingly affluent queer community. Specifically, social institutions that have historically discriminated against the LGBTQIA+ community (such as law enforcement, financial institutions, and educational institutions) are rebranded to appear queer-friendly and inclusive.

2 Cher Weixia Chen and Paul C. Gorski, "Burnout in Social Justice and Human Rights Activists: Symptoms, Causes and Implications," *Journal of Human Rights Practice* 7, no. 3 (2015): 366–90.

3 Carla Bergman and Nick Montgomery, *Joyful Militancy: Building Thriving Resistance in Toxic Times* (Chico, CA: AK Press, 2017).

4 http://deepaiyer.com/the-map-social-change-ecosystem/

5 https://www.ted.com/speakers/sarah_corbett

6 https://www.dancemagazine.com/protest-dance/

7 https://c4aa.org/

8 https://items.ssrc.org/from-our-archives/what-is-activist-research/

9 See Julene Siddique and Rae Johnson, "Accessing the Untapped Resource of Humankind through Critical Cultural Action and Embodied Arts Praxis," *Eruditio* 3, no. 1 (2021): 41–57.

10 Augusto Boal and S. Epstein, "The Cop in the Head: Three Hypotheses," *Tulane Drama Review* 34, no. 3 (1990): 35.

11 adrienne maree brown, *Emergent Strategy* (Chico, CA: AK Press, 2017), 17.

12 See chapter 4 for references and additional specifics.

13 See, for example: Bessel van der Kolk, "Posttraumatic Stress Disorder and the Nature of Trauma," *Dialogues in Clinical Neuroscience* 2, no. 1 (2000): 7–22; and Pat Ogden, "The Different Impact of Trauma and Relational Stress on Physiology, Posture, and Movement: Implications for Treatment," *European Journal of Trauma and Dissociation* 5, no. 4 (2021): 100172.

14 One such model is the Resilience Toolkit, which can be found at https:// lumostransforms.com/.

15 See, for example, Yuri Terasawa et al., "Interoceptive Sensitivity Predicts Sensitivity to the Emotions of Others," *Cognition and Emotion* 28, no. 8 (2014): 1435–48.

16 Every effort has been made to refer to ethnicity, race, and gender in an inclusive and fair way in this book. In keeping with current practices and in alignment with the National Association of Black Journalists, I have chosen to capitalize the word White when referring to race, in order to avoid framing Whiteness as the standard, and to recognize how Whiteness functions in our institutions and communities. I have also chosen to capitalize the terms Black and Indigenous to signify their importance as markers of ethnicity, nationality, and community.

17 *Somatic* is a term coined by existential phenomenologist and bodywork practitioner Thomas Hanna to refer to the inner felt experience of our own bodies. This subjective experience of the body is in sharp contrast to mainstream Western perspectives on the body, which typically view the body from the outside, as a physical object. See Hanna's *Bodies in Revolt* (1970, Freeperson Press) for more on the philosophical foundations of a somatic perspective.

18 Dan Siegel's "window of tolerance" framework suggests that individuals have a typical comfort range on the spectrum of emotional intensity. When circumstances push us past our window of tolerance, we may react automatically by shutting down, lashing out, or attempting to appease. See, for example, F. M. Corrigan, J. J. Fisher, and D. J. Nutt, "Autonomic Dysregulation and the Window of Tolerance Model of the Effects of Complex Emotional Trauma," *Journal of Psychopharmacology* 25, no. 1 (2011): 17–25.

19 For more on the master's tools, see https://www.activistgraduateschool.org /on-the-masters-tools.

20 See David Abram, *The Spell of the Sensuous: Perception and Language in a More-Than-Human World* (New York: Vintage, 2012).

21 The Golden Rule, found in all major religions and almost every ethical tradition, refers to the principle of treating others as one would like to be treated. It has been endorsed by the 1993 "Declaration toward a Global Ethic" (https://www.global-ethic.org/declaration-toward-a-global-ethic/). A definition of *ubuntu* can be found at https://www.ttbook.org/interview/i-am-because-we-are-african-philosophy-ubuntu. For further reading, see: J. Ogude, ed., *Ubuntu and the Reconstitution of Community* (Indianapolis: Indiana University Press, 2019).

22 Diana Taylor, *Disappearing Acts* (Durham, NC: Duke University Press, 1997).

2. Our Body Stories

1 Jerome Bruner, "Narratives of Human Plight: A Conversation with Jerome Bruner," in *Stories Matter,* edited by Rita Charon and Martha Montello (New York: Routledge, 2004), 17–23.

2 F. Michael Connelly and D. Jean Clandinin, "Stories of Experience and Narrative Inquiry," *Educational Researcher* 19, no. 5 (1990): 2–14.

3 Brené Brown, "The Power of Vulnerability," TED, 2009, video, 20:03, https://www.ted.com/talks/brene_brown_the_power_of_vulnerability.

4 Saskia S. L. Mol et al., "Symptoms of Post-traumatic Stress Disorder after Non-traumatic Events: Evidence from an Open Population Study," *British Journal of Psychiatry* 186, no. 6 (2005): 494–99.

5 Ibrahim A. Kira et al., "Advances in Continuous Traumatic Stress Theory: Traumatogenic Dynamics and Consequences of Intergroup Conflict: The Palestinian Adolescents Case," *Psychology* 4, no. 4 (2013): 396.

6 Gillian O'Shea Brown, "Trauma and the Body," in *Healing Complex Posttraumatic Stress Disorder* (Cham, Switzerland: Springer, 2021), 77–90.

7 Bessel A. Van der Kolk, "The Body Keeps the Score: Memory and the Evolving Psychobiology of Posttraumatic Stress," *Harvard Review of Psychiatry* 1, no. 5 (1994): 253–65.

8 "Alex" is a pseudonym, and their story is shared here with permission. Identifying details have been changed or omitted to protect their privacy.

9   See the "Community Resources" section in the last chapter for some resources on writing from the body.

10   If considering your social privilege—and we all have *some*—is new territory for you, I recommend Peggy MacIntosh's work on unpacking the invisible knapsack of white privilege; it's widely available online. While the article focuses on MacIntosh's realization of the connection between white privilege and male privilege, connections between other forms of social privilege are relatively easy to make using the process she describes.

11   See D. Gastaldo et al., "Body-Map Storytelling as Research: Methodological Considerations for Telling the Stories of Undocumented Workers through Body Mapping," 2012, http://www.migrationhealth.ca/undocumented -workers-ontario/body-mapping; A. Fidyk, "Body Maps as Ecological, Affective, Relational, and Decolonizing Method," *Journal of the Canadian Association for Curriculum Studies* 18, no. 1 (2020): 123–26; and H. N. MacGregor, "Mapping the Body: Tracing the Personal and the Political Dimensions of HIV/AIDS in Khayelitsha, South Africa," *Anthropology and Medicine* 16, no. 1 (2009): 85–95.

12   Rae Johnson, "Body Stories: Researching and Performing the Embodied Experience of Oppression," in Jennifer Frank Tantia, ed., *The Art and Science of Embodied Research Design: Concepts, Methods, and Cases* (New York: Routledge, 2020), 189–99.

3. Coming to Our Senses

1   Yasuo Yuasa, *The Body: Toward an Eastern Mind-Body Theory* (Albany: SUNY Press, 1987).

2   Allan G. Johnson, *Privilege, Power, and Difference* (Mountain View, CA: Mayfield Publishing, 2001), 184.

3   Maurice Merleau-Ponty, *Phenomenology of Perception* (New York: Routledge, 2013), 408.

4   According to educational theorists Wilfred Carr and Stephen Kemmis, praxis is "not simply action based on reflection. It is action which embodies certain qualities. These include a commitment to human well-being and the search for truth, and respect for others. It is the action of people who are free, who are able to act for themselves." Wilfred Carr and Stephen Kemmis, *Becoming Critical: Education Knowledge and Action Research* (New York: Routledge, 2003).

5 Janet Price and Margrit Shildrick, eds., *Feminist Theory and the Body: A Reader* (Abingdon-on-Thames, UK: Taylor & Francis, 1999).

6 Martin Aylward, *Awake Where You Are: The Art of Embodied Awareness* (New York: Wisdom Publications, 2021).

7 For more background on recent developments in the neuroscience of embodiment, see Kim Armstrong, "Interoception: How We Understand Our Body's Inner Sensations," *APS Observer* 32, no. 8 (September 25, 2019): https://www.psychologicalscience.org/observer/interoception-how-we-understand-our-bodys-inner-sensations; and Yuta Katsumi, Karen Quigley, and Lisa Feldman Barrett, "Situating Allostasis and Interoception at the Core of Human Brain Function," *PsyArXiv* (October 3, 2021), https://doi.org/10.31234/osf.io/wezv8.

8 H. D. Critchley and S. N. Garfinkel, "Interoception and Emotion," *Current Opinion in Psychology* 17 (2017): 7–14.

9 By "witnessing," I don't mean to suggest a quality of objective, impartial consciousness that separates itself from bodily sensations as if it were trying to analyze or rise above them. Instead, I am referring here to a quality of attention that is curious about those sensations and willing to be with them—interested in where they might lead us or how they might evolve.

10 https://osher.ucsf.edu/sites/osher.ucsf.edu/files/inline-files/MAIA-2.pdf

11 Albertyna Paciorek and Lina Skora, "Vagus Nerve Stimulation as a Gateway to Interoception," *Frontiers in Psychology* 11 (2020): 1659.

12 Mirka Knaster, *Discovering the Body's Wisdom* (New York: Bantam, 2010).

4. Rewriting Body Language

1 Paul Ekman, "Emotional and Conversational Nonverbal Signals," in *Language, Knowledge, and Representation,* ed. J. M. Larrazabal and L. A. P. Miranda (Dordrecht: Springer, 2004), 9–50.

2 David B. Buller, Judee K. Burgoon, and William Gill Woodall, *Nonverbal Communication: The Unspoken Dialogue* (New York: Harper Collins, 1996).

3 Michael Argyle, *Bodily Communication* (New York: Routledge, 2013).

4 Nina-Jo Moore, M. Hickson, and D. W. Stacks, *Nonverbal Communication* (New York: Oxford University Press, 2010).

5 Joan Kellerman, James Lewis, and James D. Laird, "Looking and Loving: The Effects of Mutual Gaze on Feelings of Romantic Love," *Journal of Research in Personality* 23, no. 2 (1989): 145–61.

6 It's important to note that not all individuals (even those from the same culture) feel equally comfortable with eye contact. Those on the autism spectrum, for example, may find direct eye contact overstimulating, so we need to take neurodiversity as well as cultural diversity into account when trying to understand someone's oculesic behavior.

7 Tiffany Field, *Touch* (Cambridge, MA: MIT Press, 2014).

8 Martin S. Remland, Tricia S. Jones, and Heidi Brinkman, "Interpersonal Distance, Body Orientation, and Touch: Effects of Culture, Gender, and Age," *Journal of Social Psychology* 135, no. 3 (1995): 281–97.

9 Edward Twitchell Hall, *The Hidden Dimension* (Garden City, NY: Doubleday, 1966).

10 Judee K. Burgoon and Norah E. Dunbar, "Nonverbal Expressions of Dominance and Power in Human Relationships," in *Sage Handbook of Nonverbal Communication,* ed. V. Manusov and M. L. Patterson (Thousand Oaks, CA: Sage, 2006), 279–97.

11 Nancy Henley and Jo Freeman, "The Sexual Politics of Interpersonal Behavior," in *Women: A Feminist Perspective,* ed. Jo Freeman (Oakland, CA: Mayfield Publishing, 1984): 391–401.

12 Robert Sommer, *Personal Space: The Behavioral Basis of Design* (Englewood Cliffs, NJ: Prentice Hall, 1969).

13 Steve L. Ellyson and John F. Dovidio, eds., *Power, Dominance, and Nonverbal Behavior* (New York: Springer Science and Business Media, 2012).

14 Shulamith Firestone, "The Dialectic of Sex," in *Radical Feminism: A Documentary Reader* (New York: NYU Press, 2000), 90–97.

15 Henley and Freeman, "Sexual Politics."

16 Christine Caldwell, PhD, BC-DMT, LPC, is the founder of and professor emeritus in the Somatic Counseling Program at Naropa University in Boulder, Colorado, USA, where she taught coursework in somatic counseling theory and skills, clinical neuroscience, research, and diversity issues. Her work began forty years ago with studies in anthropology, dance therapy, bodywork, and Gestalt therapy; since then it has developed into innovations in the field of body-centered psychotherapy. She calls her work the Moving Cycle. This system goes beyond the limitations of therapy and emphasizes lifelong personal and social evolution through trusting and following body states. The

Moving Cycle spotlights natural play, early physical imprinting, and the transformational effect of fully sequenced movement processes. She has taught at the University of Maryland, George Washington University, Concordia, Seoul Women's University, Southwestern College, Pacifica, and Santa Barbara Graduate Institute, and she trains, teaches, and lectures internationally. She has published over thirty articles and chapters, and her books include *Getting Our Bodies Back, Getting in Touch, The Body and Oppression,* and *Bodyfulness.*

5. Reshaping Body Image

1 This chapter has been adapted from: Rae Johnson, "Queering/Querying the Body: Sensation and Curiosity in Disrupting Body Norms," in *Oppression and the Body* (Berkeley, CA: North Atlantic Books, 2018), 97–111.

2 Kenneth B. Clark and Mamie P. Clark, "Emotional Factors in Racial Identification and Preference in Negro Children," *Journal of Negro Education* 19, no. 3 (1950): 341–50.

3 Nikki Sullivan, "Transmogrification: (Un)Becoming Other(s)," in *The Transgender Studies Reader,* ed. S. Stryker and S. Whittle (London: Routledge, 2006), 552–64.

4 David Halperin, *Saint Foucault: Towards a Gay Hagiography* (Cambridge, UK: Oxford University Press, 1997), 62.

5 Emma Hardy, "Queer Aesthetics: Not Feeling Queer Enough," *Archer,* April 11, 2017, http://archermagazine.com.au/2017/04/queer-aesthetics-not-feeling-queer-enough/.

6 Nikki Sullivan, *A Critical Introduction to Queer Theory* (New York: NYU Press, 2003), 553.

7 The following section is drawn from: Rae Johnson, *Embodied Social Justice* (New York: Routledge, 2017). Used with permission.

6. Activism in Embodied Relationship

1 bell hooks, *All about Love: New Visions* (New York: Harper Perennial, 2001).

2 https://www.ucl.ac.uk/racism-racialisation/transcript-conversation-ruth-wilson-gilmore

3   See, for example: Pier Francesco Ferrari and Vittorio Gallese, "Mirror Neurons and Intersubjectivity," *Advances in Consciousness Research* 68 (2007): 73. There is also some support in the research literature for the notion that our awareness of feeling in our own bodies (interoceptive sensitivity) is correlated with an enhanced capacity for empathy. See, for example: Yuri Terasawa et al., "Interoceptive Sensitivity Predicts Sensitivity to the Emotions of Others," *Cognition and Emotion* 28, no. 8 (2014): 1435–48.

4   Gail Weiss, *Body Images: Embodiment as Intercorporeality* (New York: Routledge, 2013), 5.

5   There is increasing evidence that emotions are somatosensory events (not cognitive ones) and that we experience emotions in our body in much the same locations (hands, face, chest, pelvis, etc.) as others do. See, for example: Sofia Volynets et al., "Bodily Maps of Emotions are Culturally Universal," *Emotion* 20, no. 7 (2020): 1127. Also: Lauri Nummenmaa et al., "Bodily Maps of Emotions," *Proceedings of the National Academy of Sciences* 111, no. 2 (2014): 646–51.

6   Niki Koumoutsos et al., "Embodying Social Justice: Reshaping Implicit Biases with Gendlin's Implicit Precision," Emergent Dialogue & Focusing, https://www.emergentdialogue.com/docs/endorsements/embod-social-justice-abstract.pdf.

7   This section is adapted from a previously published article: Rae Johnson, Lucia Leighton, and Christine Caldwell, "The Embodied Experience of Microaggressions: Implications for Clinical Practice," *Journal of Multicultural Counseling and Development* 46, no. 3 (2018): 156–70. Used with permission.

8   Derald Wing Sue, *Microaggressions in Everyday Life: Race, Gender, and Sexual Orientation* (Hoboken, NJ: John Wiley & Sons, 2010), xvi.

9   Cornel West, "Justice Is What Love Looks Like in Public," lecture, Howard University, Washington, DC, April 11, 2011, video, 1:00:00, https://www.youtube.com/watch?v=nGqP7S_WO6o.

10 Rushworth M. Kidder and Bruce McLeod, *Moral Courage* (New York: William Morrow, 2005).

11 Bessel A. Van der Kolk, *The Body Keeps the Score: Brain, Mind, and Body in the Healing of Trauma* (New York: Penguin Books, 2015).

12 Robin DiAngelo, *White Fragility: Why It's So Hard for White People to Talk about Racism* (Boston: Beacon Press, 2018).

13 Sam Grant, PhD, is a lifelong organizer who works at the intersections of cultural, economic, and environmental justice. He has cofounded many organizations and initiatives, including AfroEco, Full Circle Community Institute, Organizing Apprenticeship Project, the Wendell Phillips Community Development Federal Credit Union, the Green Institute Eco-Industrial Park, and the Grassroots Public Policy Institute, among others. He has been on faculty at Metropolitan State University since 1990 and has trained thousands of social justice facilitators around the world. He is currently executive director of Rainbow Research, a national social justice research and evaluation firm, and is cofounder with his wife and friends of Embody Deep Democracy, an international worker cooperative.

14 Danusha Laméris, "Small Kindnesses," from *Bonfire Opera* (Pittsurgh: University of Pittsburgh Press, 2020). Reprinted by permission of University of Pittsburgh Press.

15 Mary Whitehouse, "The Tao of the Body" (Los Angeles: Analytical Psychology Club of Los Angeles, 1958).

16 Try thinking of inanimate forms as also having bodies; clouds have bodies, lakes have bodies, flowers have bodies, and so on.

7. Bringing It All Home

1 bell hooks, *Teaching to Transgress* (New York: Routledge, 2014), 34.

2 Audre Lorde, *Burst of Light* (London: Women's Press, 1992).

3 To download a copy of Iyer's guide, go to https://buildingmovement.org /wp-content/uploads/2020/06/Final-Mapping-Ecosystem-Guide-CC -BY-NC-SA-4.0-Handles.pdf.

4 Thanks to Cate Denial for her innovative work on human asset maps. See https://catherinedenial.org/blog/uncategorized/human-asset-maps -encouraging-social-justice-work-in-my-students/.

5 You can also create an embodied resilience map using an outline of your body, as you did with the embodied asset map. On the outline of your body, decide where to note the various components—perhaps the emotional domain in the heart area and the intellectual domain in the head area— but where these domains go should reflect where you actually do feel these demands and resources in your body.

6 The list of community resources provided in chapter 7 is necessarily limited and incomplete. Inclusion on this list does not constitute an endorsement by the author, and exclusion from the list simply reflects the limits of my current knowledge and existing space constraints.

Index

About the Author

 RAE JOHNSON, PhD, RSW, RSMT, BCC, is a social worker, somatic movement therapist, and scholar/activist working at the intersections of embodiment and social justice. Rae's approach to embodied activism has been shaped by decades of frontline work with street youth, women in addiction recovery, psychiatric survivors, and members of the queer community. Since completing their doctoral studies, Rae has held academic positions in several somatic psychology programs, including at Naropa University and Pacifica Graduate Institute. They currently teach somatic psychology at the California Institute of Integral Studies and codirect an online certificate program in embodied activism.

About North Atlantic Books

North Atlantic Books (NAB) is an independent, nonprofit publisher committed to a bold exploration of the relationships between mind, body, spirit, and nature. Founded in 1974, NAB aims to nurture a holistic view of the arts, sciences, humanities, and healing. To make a donation or to learn more about our books, authors, events, and newsletter, please visit www.northatlanticbooks.com.